Setting the Record Straight

Setting the Record Straight

Responses to Misconceptions About Public Education in the U.S.

Second Edition

Gerald W. Bracey

HEINEMANN ■ Portsmouth, NH

Heinemann
A division of Reed Elsevier Inc.
361 Hanover Street
Portsmouth, NH 03801–3912
www.heinemann.com

Offices and agents throughout the world

The first edition of this book was published in 1997 by the Association for Supervision and Curriculum Development.

The author and publisher wish to thank those who have generously given permission to reprint borrowed material:

Figure 10–1: "Iowa Tests of Basic Skills National Norming Data Trends, 1955–2000." Reprinted by permission of Iowa Testing Programs, University of Iowa.

Figure 15–2: "Unequal School Funding in the United States." Reprinted by permission of Bruce Biddle and David Berliner.

Library of Congress Cataloging-in-Publication Data
Bracey, Gerald W. (Gerald Watkins)
  Setting the record straight : responses to misconceptions about public education in the U.S. / Gerald W. Bracey. — 2nd ed.
    p. cm.
  Includes bibliographical references.
  ISBN 0-325-00594-X (alk. paper)
    1. Public schools—United States. 2. Academic achievement—United States.
3. Education—United States—Finance. I. Title.

LA217.2.B73 2004
371.01'0973—dc22   2004010979

Editor: Lois Bridges
Production: Vicki Kasabian
Cover design: Jenny Jensen Greenleaf
Typesetter: Tom Allen, Pear Graphic Design
Manufacturing: Steve Bernier

Printed in the United States of America on acid-free paper
08 07 06 05 04 VP 1 2 3 4 5

For Iris and Teddie, of course,
and Raki, the dog (not the liquor for which he is named),
whose long walks in the marina park allowed me
to think about the data in surroundings
other than the computer-staled air of my office.

# Contents

Acknowledgments

Thanks to various members of the Education Policy Studies Laboratory at Arizona State University for counsel and encouragement and data. And thanks also to Heinemann editor Lois Bridges, whose unflagging enthusiasm helped me keep going.

Why People Need This Book

People in education need this book because of the War Against America's Public Schools, to borrow from the title of another book I authored. Various groups have various motives for engaging public schools in combat. Conservatives and free-market theorists push the privatization of public schools. Some people genuinely believe that vouchers children could use at any school, not just the one in their neighborhood, would induce competition among schools and this in turn would improve the system overall. Good schools would thrive, poor schools would close. The reality is more complicated and there is no evidence to date that events would play out as market theorists hope.

Some from the Christian Right would like a privatized system in which they could teach religion without crashing against the First Amendment wall separating church and state. Catholic educators, whose schools have been hemorrhaging students— Catholic schools contained 12 percent of all students forty years ago, 4 percent today—would no doubt favor such a system as well. They had maintained a discrete silence on the matter, but since the Supreme Court declared the Cleveland program constitutional, they have openly lobbied for vouchers (67 percent of the students using vouchers in Cleveland attend Catholic schools; 96 percent attend some church-affiliated school).

Liberals and some professors at research universities abet the war. Liberals usually support public schools and want more resources for them. To obtain these resources, they emphasize the problems, not the accomplishments, of schools. Indeed, I was once disinvited to speak at a state conference because the legislature was considering additional monies and educators worried that if I showed that schools were doing better than people thought, the legislature might vote no. Bill Clinton used to say often that only 40 percent of our third graders could read independently. The basis for this claim is questionable, but he could have said instead that among students from twenty-seven nations, American third graders finished second in a study of reading skills. Instead, he focused on the negative.

The psychology of things-are-dire-so-we-need-more-money-for-the-schools also afflicts educational researchers. Many university appointments depend on soft money—money from grants. Professors increase their chances of liberating money from foundations and the federal and state governments by pointing to problems that need solving.

There are also those who would destroy public schools with a threefold political agenda: First, putting schools in private hands would benefit corporate America. Second, ending public education would shrink the public sector, a goal of some on the Right. Third, two organizations that contribute money and many votes for Democrats—the teachers unions—would also lose power and perhaps even fold. Vouchers and privatization, to some, are means to increase the power and control of the Republican party.

Finally, some people look at the $800,000,000,000 a year (yes, that's eight hundred billion) that the United States spends on all types of education and want some of the pot. Elementary and secondary education, which account for about $400 billion, constitute the last large existing markets mostly untapped by for-profits. Entrepreneurs have already privatized hospitals and jails. Of course, the state of our health and penal systems might give some people pause before inflicting the same "solution" on schools (in a 2003 Gallup confidence poll, people ranked HMOs as the least trusted of all institutions).

> *To date, efforts to operate public schools for a profit have largely failed.*

To date, efforts to operate public schools for a profit have largely failed. The first firm to actively pursue money in schools, TesseracT (née, Educational Alternatives), went bankrupt in 2000, and at the time of writing, the largest such existing firm, Edison Schools, had lost money in all but one quarter in its twelve-year history. It went public in 1999 but was taken private again in 2003. Of the other firms that manage public schools, only two turn a profit (neither is a publicly held company). One, National Heritage Academies of Michigan, caters to a niche market and pays teachers poorly. The other, White Hat Management in Ohio, also pays teachers poorly but seems to survive largely because its CEO has political clout rather than because its schools offer educational benefits.

People in schools need to arm themselves with the data in this book.

People not affiliated with the schools—parents, grandparents, concerned citizens—need to know what the data actually say about the health of the school system. This they certainly will not find in the national media. The old journalism saw "If it bleeds, it leads" applies double to stories about schools, even leading to the publication of erroneous data on occasion. Although most people do not have school-age children, schools affect everyone, not just parents. It is today's eighteen-year-olds whose contributions to Social Security will support today's fifty-year-olds. Or not. Children are the future.

> *The old journalism saw "If it bleeds, it leads" applies double to stories about schools, even leading to the publication of erroneous data on occasion.*

The Media's Role in the War on Public Schools

"Japanese Students Second, American Students Next to Last"

If American and Japanese students took a test and American kids scored higher, this is the headline I would predict. It is factually correct. With only two countries in the race, the first-place American kids would also rank next to last.

Sometimes I think all reporters must have had terrible experiences in school and are working through their early traumas in print or just using their jobs for payback. Media tend to accentuate the negative generally, but they overdo it for schools. When the National Assessment of Educational Progress (NAEP) geography results appeared, *Washington Post* reporter Michael Fletcher called them, for no good reason, "dismal." When I complained to another *Post* reporter about that word, the other reporter said that modern journalism practice requires writers to call attention to articles by jazzing them up.

The media ignore good news and splash bad news across the

front page. In February 1992, an international study in mathematics and science found American students ranked mostly, but not entirely, low, although scores were average. The media gave the report a lot of attention. "An 'F' in World Competition" was the headline over the *Newsweek* story. In July 1992, an international study on reading found American students second in the world among twenty-seven nations. No coverage except for the Binghamton (New York) *Press and Sun-Bulletin*; the person who directed the U.S. portion of the study teaches at State University of New York at Binghamton and no doubt had called the newspaper.

The media have had help, of course. Under Ronald Reagan and Bush I and II, the U.S. Department of Education pushed vouchers and tuition tax credits. As one strategy for that agenda, it hyped bad news and ignored—or suppressed—good news.

More difficult to understand was the differential treatment the press gave the results of NAEP geography and history assessments in 1995. U.S. Department of Education officials Laurence Ogle and Patricia Dabbs attended press conferences on the release of both sets of data. They reported that the "mood of almost all speakers was clearly upbeat" at the geography press release.[1] The reporting in the press, however, was lackluster and negative at best. Few news agencies picked up the story. Maybe that's a good thing: those that did blew it. Even *Education Week,* which bills itself as "American Education's Newspaper of Record," got the record wrong and confabulated bad news. It headlined the story as "Students Fall Short in NAEP Geography Test."[2]

The *Washington Post* labeled the results of the history assessment "dismal" (*dismal* is a favorite term among education reporters), while *Harper's* editor Lewis Lapham declared them a "coroner's report." The contrast between the geography and the history coverage startled Ogle and Dabbs. When they got back to their offices after the history press conference, "[they] found [their] voice-mail jam-packed with media accounts for additional information" (this was prior to heavy use of e-mail). Coverage was widespread. "Even television's late night comedy king, Jay Leno, spoke about (and ridiculed) the results. Clearly, the coverage of the negative news (about history) eclipsed the relatively good news about geography."

And then there's PIRLS—Progress in International Reading Literacy Study—released in April 2003 and covered by virtually no one. Only four papers had bylined stories and about fifteen carried an AP wire story.[3] American students finished ninth overall among thirty-five nations and only three nations had significantly higher scores. PIRLS is discussed in more detail on pages 165–168.

As disturbing as the emphasis on the negative is the lack of analytic, critical reporting. Journalists, after all, are *supposed* to be skeptical. Too often, they aren't. The late Richard Harwood, ombudsman for the *Washington Post,* wrote that "between 70 and 90 percent of our [journalists'] content is at heart the voice of officials and their experts, translated by reporters into supposedly 'objective' news."[4] No wonder, then, that when Joseph Reaves of Arizona State University analyzed editorial coverage of George W. Bush's No Child Left Behind legislation—which I have characterized as a weapon of mass destruction—he titled his report *Falling in Line.* [5]

Getting the Word Out to Parents
A 1994 survey by the American Association of School Administrators found that Americans get most of their news about the nation's schools from television and newspapers. They get most of their information about local schools from local sources. Little wonder, then, that Americans simultaneously think that the local schools are OK and that the nation's schools stink. If school folk want Americans to know that the nation's schools are not in such dire straits, they should start putting the national and international statistics in this book in the newsletters schools send home. Given the media's focus on the negative, that's the only way people will find out what is the true condition of American education.

Two Excellent Additional Resources

Kaplan, George R. 1992. *Images of Education: The Mass Media's Version of America's Schools.* Washington, DC: Institute for Educational Leadership.

Maeroff, Gene I., ed. 1998. *Imaging Education: The Media and Schools in America.* New York: Teachers College Press. (See especially David C. Berliner and Bruce J. Biddle's "The Lamentable Alliance Between the Media and School Critics," 26–45.)

Notes

1. Ogle, Laurence, and Patricia Dabbs. 1996. "Good News, Bad News: Does Media Coverage of Schools Promote Scattershot Remedies?" *Education Week* (13 March): 46.

2. Lawton, Millicent. 1995. "Students Fall Short in NAEP Geography Test." *Education Week* (25 October).

3. Ogle, Laurence, and Patricia Dabbs. 1996. "Good News, Bad News: Does Media Coverage of Schools Promote Scattershot Remedies?" *Education Week* (13 March): 46.

4. Harwood, Richard. 1994. "Reporting On, By, and For an Elite." *Washington Post*, 28 May, A21.

5. Reaves, Joseph. 2002. *Falling in Line: An Examination of Editorials Appearing in Four Leading U.S. Newspapers from the Inauguration of George W. Bush to September 2001.* Tempe, AZ: Arizona State University, Educational Policy Research Unit, April. Available at *www.asu.edu/educ/epsl.*

Note About This Edition

I wrote the first edition of this book in 1996 and the Association for Supervision and Curriculum Development (ASCD) published it in early 1997. This revision of *Setting the Record Straight* puts in one place all of the current data that bear on the myths that the first edition debunked. The data still lead to the same conclusions reached in the first edition, but more recent studies have superceded much of what was in the 1997 book.

In terms of data replacement, the space given in the first edition to the Second International Assessment of Educational Progress in mathematics and science of 1992 has been reallocated to the more recent Third International Mathematics and Science Study of 1995 (reported in 1996, 1997, and 1998), the Third International Mathematics and Science Study–Repeat (1999, reported in 2001), the Program of International Student Assessment (1999, reported in 2001), and the Progress in Reading Literacy Study (2001, reported in 2003).

Similarly, when *Setting the Record Straight* was written in 1996, few data existed on an increasingly popular innovation, charter schools. Minnesota passed the first charter school law in 1991. By 1996, twenty-four other states had joined the movement, but advocates had created only four hundred schools and no researchers had evaluated the outcomes. In the ensuing years, the number of charters has grown to three thousand, and evaluators have conducted both state-level and national studies. In 2003 alone, three evaluations of California charters appeared, as did one quasi-national evaluation and one summary of other evaluations.

When *Setting the Record Straight* was written, the only evaluations of any voucher programs were those officially commissioned by the state of Wisconsin to look at the Milwaukee voucher program. The first edition reported the results of John Witte's fifth-year evaluation of the Milwaukee voucher project,[1] but Jay P. Greene and Paul E. Peterson's inflammatory op-ed in the

Wall Street Journal (it carried the title "Choice Data Rescued from Bad Science"[2]) rejecting Witte's analysis had not yet appeared, nor had any evaluation data appeared on the Cleveland voucher program, which the Ohio legislature had authorized in 1995. Vouchers were very much in the political air but voucher data were yet to be unearthed. The data that have arrived in the ensuing years do not show vouchers as a viable, effective tool for education reform and these results are detailed in Chapter 9.

Finally, when the first edition of this book appeared, neither Sandy Kress, nor Karl Rove, nor George W. Bush had dreamed up No Child Left Behind. It is treated in Chapter 6.

Notes

1. Witte, John D., T. D. Sterr, and C. A. Thorn. 1995. *Fifth Year Evaluation Report: Milwaukee Choice Program.* Madison, WI: Department of Political Science, University of Wisconsin.

2. Greene, Jay P., Paul E. Peterson, and Jiangtao Du. 1996. "Choice Data Rescued from Bad Science." *Wall Street Journal,* 14 August, A14.

Setting the Record Straight

ntroduction

Bad news about American public schools is a cognitive neutrino. Physical neutrinos are subatomic particles with no mass or charge. They pass through you by the millions each day but you don't notice. That's the way bad news about schools works for most people. We read the headline, note the negative story, and go on with our business. Cognitive neutrino.

If asked, we will say that the local schools are OK, but there's a crisis in education, nationally speaking. We read it in the papers. The papers, of course, are cursed with a different affliction: the neurotic need to believe the worst. If it's bad news, it's not, as we shall see several times, even worth checking the facts to corroborate. It must be true. If it's good news, it is to be ignored or dismissed as resulting from some exceptional circumstance.

But, despite the almost unremitting criticism of public schools, trust in public schools remains little changed. Forty-three percent of the public said they trusted public schools in 1990; 40 percent said so in 2003.[1, 2] Cognitive neutrinos. In fact, people trust public schools more than the institutions that are trying to fix them. In 2003, newspapers garnered 33 percent confidence, Congress 29 percent, and big business 22 percent. Makes you wonder who should be reforming whom, doesn't it?

> *But, despite the almost unremitting criticism of public schools, trust in public schools remains little changed. Forty-three percent of the public said they trusted public schools in 1990; 40 percent said so in 2003.*

This persistent criticism of schools began with the onset of the Cold War soon after World War II ended in 1945. The steady stream of negativity probably accounts for much of our openness to negativity. At that time, politicians, generals, defense specialists, and university professors came to see schools for the first time as integral to national defense and, at the same time, as lacking. In Russia, it was said, twice as many engineers, scientists, and mathematicians labored feverishly on weapons and space technology as in the United States.

Where would we get the manpower we needed? Well, from the universities, of course. But where would the universities get their students? From the schools. Some unsystematic examinations by American observers, especially Admiral Hyman Rickover, father of the nuclear navy, concluded that existing schools were not up to the task. Rickover stumped the country saying, "Let us never forget that there can be no second place in a contest with Russia and that there will be no second chance if we lose."[3]

Typical of the harsh post–World War II criticism was the severe tongue-lashing delivered to schools and especially schools of education by historian Arthur Bestor in his influential 1953 book, *Educational Wastelands: The Retreat from Learning in Our Public Schools.*[4] The presence of the word *retreat* in the title is significant. It is one of the earliest, perhaps the first, statements expressing the sentiment that things used to be better. This false nostalgia for some golden age of American education when everyone learned to high levels remains widespread even today.

When, in 1957, the Russians launched *Sputnik,* the first man-made satellite to orbit Earth, the school bashers felt vindicated. *Sputnik* proved they had been right all along. The schools never really recovered from *Sputnik.* Twelve years after *Sputnik,* America put a man on the Moon, a heavenly body that the Russians, for all their vaunted technological superiority, couldn't even *hit.* As the Eisenhower "togetherness" fifties gave way to the sex, drugs, and rock 'n' roll sixties of John F. Kennedy and Lyndon Johnson, many books excoriated schools as places where students' minds and spirits died. Jonathan Kozol's 1967 *Death at an Early Age* was typical.[5] In 1970, another influential book, Charles Silberman's *Crisis in the Classroom,* shook educators again.[6] Silberman early acknowledged that 176 out of 186 studies comparing test scores "then and now" found test scores higher now (whenever defined) than then (whenever defined). Yet, Silberman considered schools in crisis because the test scores concealed their ghastly character:

> Because adults take schools so much for granted, they fail to appreciate what grim, joyless places most American schools are, how oppressive and petty are the rules by which they're gov-

erned, how intellectually sterile and aesthetically barren, what an appalling lack of civility obtains on the part of teachers and principals, what contempt they conspicuously display for children as children. (10)

Without question, the most celebrated negative news report about schools was 1983's *A Nation at Risk,* often referred to as "the paper *Sputnik.*"[7] Some people still call it a landmark study and when its twentieth anniversary rolled around in April 2003, several articles and reports claimed the country was still at risk.[8, 9, 10, 11] I disagreed.[12]

The National Commission on Excellence in Education, convened by then Secretary of Education Terrel Bell, had produced the report. Knowing that commission reports often languish on shelves, Bell's commissioners did something smart. They hired professional writers. As a consequence, the report flowed with rhetorical flourishes like this:

> Our nation is at risk. Our once unchallenged preeminence in commerce, industry, science, and technological innovation is being overtaken by competitors throughout the world . . . the educational foundations of our society are presently being eroded by a rising tide of mediocrity that threatens our very future as a Nation and a people. . . . If an unfriendly foreign power had attempted to impose on America the mediocre educational performance that exists today, we might well have viewed it as an act of war. (7)

Rising tide of mediocrity? Act of war? Tough words, strong rhetoric (rhetoric not justified by the facts that underpinned it, or didn't).[13] *A Nation at Risk* launched a whole new round of educational reforms that quickly headed off in a new direction. After *Sputnik,* reformers proposed new, more modern, more powerful curricula. We needed "teacher-proof" instructional materials that could "speak directly to the child." Such materials were disasters, but the idea was to *fix* the schools.

A Nation at Risk followed in this line of thought by calling for more: more hours in the school day, more days in the school year, more technology, more math and science courses, more rigorous courses, more and more professionally trained teachers. Not long after *A Nation at Risk* appeared, though, demands came not for *more* but for *different*. We needed to restructure schools, reformers said. Calls for reform led to shouts for doing away with the public schools altogether. Schools need competition. Privatize them. Give kids vouchers to attend any school that will accept the vouchers as payment.

The years following the publication of *A Nation at Risk* have witnessed an unprecedented outpouring of anti–public school sentiments, often expressed by people who were putatively charged with improving them. Former U.S. Department of Education officials Chester E. Finn Jr., Diane Ravitch, Lamar Alexander, and William J. Bennett form a virtual chorus line singing the sins of public schools and extolling the virtues of their privatized alternatives (Bennett currently chairs a private, for-profit, online educational delivery service bankrolled by former junk bond king Michael Milken). And because most newspaper articles consist largely of what people in positions of authority tell the reporters,[14] their comments get wide dispersion (see "The Media's Role in the War on Public Schools," page xiii). A steady drumbeat of school failure tried to convince people that an education crisis imperiled the nation, even though those same people, whatever they thought about schools in general, believed their own schools were OK (a disconnect that should have alerted people that at least one of their conclusions was wrong).

People who were sufficiently familiar with education that they should have known better accepted erroneous or misleading data. Three incidents drove home to me the degree to which people would believe the worst about schools. I recount one incident in full in Chapter 5. Suffice it to say here that the editors at *Education Week* failed to do the proper fact checking on some SAT statistics and reported numbers that screamed failure. Their statistics showed, they thought, that in the decade following *A Nation at Risk*, despite all the talk of reform, both the number and the proportion of high scorers on the SAT had actually declined. But the *Education Week* numbers were wrong. No doubt the editors would have double-checked their figures had they indicated an increase in high scorers, but the numbers showed a decline so they had to be right because we all know the schools are lousy (the number and the proportion of SAT high scorers had actually *increased* substantially [see pages 60–66]).

The second incident occurred on my first day on the job in

Cherry Creek, Colorado schools. As I walked into my office, I noticed a green sheet of paper on the bulletin board just outside. It presented "the lists." One list catalogued the horrors in schools of the 1940s. The other, the problems of the 1980s. The first list contained such offenses as talking in class, chewing gum, making noise, running in the halls, breaking in line, and not putting paper in wastebaskets. In the 1980s, schools were afflicted with drug abuse, alcohol abuse, pregnancy, suicide, rape, robbery, and assault. The green sheet listed the Fullerton, California, Police Department as the source. Seemed like odd research for a police department, but maybe they were getting more proximate to social science.

I thought no more about the lists and have kicked myself ever since. Fortunately, when the lists turned up on a bulletin board at Yale, they sparked more interest in professor Barry O'Neill's brain than in mine. O'Neill was skeptical and sought the source.

He collected 250 versions of the lists and found that the Right and the Left had both taken them to their hearts: William Bennett, Rush Limbaugh, Phyllis Schlafly, and George Will had embraced them from the starboard, but so had Anna Quindlen, Herb Caen, and Carl Rowan from portside. The lists had appeared in *Time* and on CBS News. Their origin was variously attributed to CBS News, *CQ Researcher,* and the Heritage Foundation.

O'Neill found, though, that a single person, T. Cullen Davis of Fort Worth, Texas, had produced them. When acquitted of murdering his estranged wife's lover, Davis had had an epiphany, smashed his million-dollar collection of statuary as false idols and became a born-again Christian. Somehow, this new identity led him on a crusade against public schools. O'Neill inquired of Davis his methodology. "How did I know what the offenses in the schools were in 1940? I was there. How do I know what they are now? I read the paper."[15]

The third incident started with a column by *Washington Post* pundit William Raspberry.[16] I esteem Raspberry as one of the nation's finest columnists. One cannot categorize Raspberry as liberal or moderate or anything else. His is a uniquely independent mind. He often reasons his way to conclusions that one would not expect of a liberal or conservative writer. Reading a column, you can see him thinking, really thinking, his way to his judgments—as opposed to throwing up arguments to justify conclusions already reached.

He thus surprised me one day by reporting findings that seemed to me ludicrous on their face. Raspberry described a study wherein researchers found that ten- and twelve-year-olds could read VCR manuals better than eighteen-year-olds and that high school dropouts read the manuals better than high school graduates. Given a VCR, a manual, and a ten-minute time limit, the younger students had greater success in getting the VCR connected to a TV, setting the clock, and programming the machine to record a movie the following day. If the research had found that the younger kids were better than their *parents,* I might have accepted it.

Although I studied cognitive psychology in graduate school, I hadn't kept up with the field, so I consulted cognitive psychologists I knew all across the country. None of them had heard of the study. None of them thought the findings reasonable, although one facetiously concluded that obviously we needed to encourage more students to drop out of school and earlier.

Raspberry's source was an article by consultant Willard Daggett in *The Executive Educator,* a publication of the National School Boards Association.[17] Daggett provided no citation for the study, so I called his office. "It's an old example that he no longer uses," said someone in his office, a rather curious answer, I thought. In a letter, Daggett said he had used it only once in a speech because he had read about it the previous day in the *New York Times.* Perusing the *New York Times Index* at the local library, I found nothing (I know it's hard to believe, but these were the days before many people were on the Net, much less addicted to Google).

I mentioned the incident as a curiosity to an audience in Illinois and they broke up laughing. The Daggett videotape they sent me explained their mirth. Far from occupying an incidental niche in the talk, the VCR saga formed the six-minute keystone of an hourlong presentation. Daggett claimed that fourteen "consumer-friendly" tools were tested and "the results were the same for all 14 products in all 50 states." It was true for boys and girls alike—the younger kids did better. In fact, high school graduates, who were inferior to dropouts, did better than people with college degrees, who in turn did better than people with master's degrees. I calculated that given all of the ages and "consumer-friendly tools" involved, the study would need a *minimum* of

350,000 people (50 subjects per group x 2 genders x 5 age/education levels x 14 machines x 50 states = 350,000). How could you do a study involving 350,000 participants that no one had ever heard of?

And who conducted this study? On the videotape, Daggett simply says "Carnegie." On another, he says "Carnegie and Ford." Another search of the *New York Times Index* under those terms produced nothing. On tape he explains the phenomenon: The National Reading Teachers Association (there is no such organization) found that reading literature is a right-brained activity while reading technical material is a left-brained activity. American high schools emphasize right-brained literature, which causes the left brain to diminish in capacity (in fact, all language is processed in the left hemisphere). Would that it were that simple.

My searches produced nothing because, of course, the study existed only in Daggett's head (a common feature of his talks, I came to learn).

Consider for a moment: Daggett is a popular speaker, so we can be reasonably sure that tens of thousands of educators had sat through this fantasy. He had also managed to get it past the editors at a respectable publication, *The Executive Educator.* And he had bamboozled one of our very best pundits. How could that happen?

It could happen because bad news is like the neutrinos mentioned earlier. I have come to call the bad news nonreactions the Bad News Neutrino Syndrome. Bad news is accepted immediately, uncritically. Good news is either ignored or rejected or considered to have occurred because of some exceptional circumstance. How many people have ever heard of the study *How in the World Do Students Read?* Only those who have heard me speak, I daresay. When I report the findings of this study, I ask for a show of hands from people who know about it. Almost never over a twelve-year period has even one hand shot into the air. American kids finished second among twenty-seven nations (see pages 162–163). The U.S. Department of Education dismissed the study as irrelevant.[18]

> *Bad news is accepted immediately, uncritically. Good news is either ignored or rejected or considered to have occurred because of some exceptional circumstance.*

A similar study, Progress in International Reading Literacy Study (PIRLS), appeared in April 2003. Again, no one has heard of this study wherein only three nations among thirty-five had significantly higher scores than American kids. Only the *Boston Globe,* the *Boston Herald,* and the *Washington Times* carried bylined stories.[19, 20, 21] The *Washington Post* buried a brief AP wire story and the *New York Times* and most other papers in the nation carried not a word (PIRLS is discussed more extensively in Chapter 12).

OK, I confess: I have not always been as skeptical about bad news as I am now. I pretty much accepted *Crisis in the Classroom,* partly because I thought Silberman's solution to "the crisis"—informal education as developed in the English infant schools—was a good one. I didn't believe a lot of *A Nation at Risk,* but, hey, I had a job that kept me busy, so I didn't have time to dig into the data presented to see if they were accurate.

But, seven years after the publication of *A Nation at Risk,* a nearly chance occasion started me down the road to contrarianism. The accident that changed my professional life and led to most of what I've written about and done in the last thirteen years was a column carried in the *Denver Post* on November 4, 1990. The *Denver Post* belonged to the *Washington Post–Los Angeles Times* syndicate and reprinted selected columns. On November 4, 1990, it carried one by *Washington Post* columnist Richard Cohen, "Johnny's Miserable SATs."[22] I quickly realized that Cohen suffered some fundamental misunderstandings about the nature of the SAT that pretty much destroyed his argument, but his column piqued me to do my own analysis.

I conducted a not very sophisticated inquiry to factor out the demographic changes in who has taken the SAT since the standards were set in 1941. The standards were set on 10,654 white kids living in New England (and a few in other northeastern states). The standard setters were 98 percent white and 61 percent male, and 41 percent had attended private college-prep high schools.[23] They were an elite. It was to the average score of this elite that the College Board assigned the scaled score of 500 (the Educational Testing Service, or ETS, didn't exist yet).

The SAT test-taking pool in 1990 looked quite different from that in 1941. It consisted of more than a million kids. Fifty-two percent were female, 29 percent were minorities, and only 12 percent attended private schools of any kind. Thirty percent reported family incomes of less than $30,000 a year.

When I compared groups that seemed most like the standard setters, I found a small decline in the verbal score and a tiny increase in math. I sent my analysis to *Education Week,* which published it under the headline "SAT Scores: Miserable or Miraculous?"[24] After publication, people drew my attention to other indicators showing the same absence of decline. Most curious was a call from Lee Bray, an engineer and vice president at Sandia National Laboratories in Albuquerque. Bray said that he and a group of engineers had recently completed a large study of the educational system and had found lots of things that agreed with my analysis of SAT scores. He was coming to Denver and suggested we meet so he could show me a draft of the report.

Over dinner, we perused the document, 156 pages, each page consisting of a graph on one side and text explaining the graph on the other. Later, Bob Huelskamp, one of the engineers who had assembled the report, also came to Denver and made a presentation to my staff and me. I suggested we put what I had and what they had together and publish it somewhere, preferably in the popular press. Huelskamp said they couldn't, that they were paralyzed by "internal politics."

The engineers had ventured to Washington to make a presentation to congressional staffers and officers in the Departments of Education and Energy (the Energy Department funds Sandia). At some point, David Kearns, former CEO of Xerox and then deputy secretary of education, said, "You bury this, or I'll bury you." An article in *Education Week* said only that "administration officials, particularly Mr. Kearns, reacted angrily at the meeting." The same article also said some source, unnamed, told the engineers to keep quiet or their careers would end.[25] James Watkins, then Secretary of Energy, called the report "dead wrong" in a letter to the *Albuquerque Journal.* At some point, the engineers were forbidden to leave New Mexico to talk about their work.

The report was suppressed, although I circulated it widely, as did Larry Barber at Phi Delta Kappa. The "official story" from Diane Ravitch at the U.S. Department of Education was that the report was undergoing "peer review" and was not yet ready for publication. Lee Bray, now retired and thus impervious to any threats from political appointees at the Energy or Education

Departments, told me in 2001 that the report was definitely suppressed. It saw print only after the first Bush administration, having accentuated the negative about American public schools for four years, left town in 1992. It appeared as the entirety of the May/June 1993 issue of the *Journal of Educational Research,* where it was seen by few.[26]

Huelskamp, having declined to join me in a publication, then encouraged me to publish on my own. After all, he pointed out, the Sandia engineers had done little original research. They had mined most of the data from various government agencies—especially the U.S. Department of Education—and the data were therefore already in the public domain. Sandia had no proprietary claim to them, nor did the team members feel any need to see their names in print.

By this time, I had several other compilations of data, such as ETS's *Performance at the Top,* all suggesting that public schools were afflicted with something less than a crisis.[27] I added many of the Sandia report's findings to what I already had and published them in *Phi Delta Kappan* as "Why Can't They Be Like We Were?"[28] The title was the first of numerous attempts to dispel the false nostalgia that there once was a golden age of American public education when everyone learned to high levels. It's a snippet of a lyric from the 1960 musical *Bye Bye Birdie:* "Why can't they be like we were, perfect in every way? Oh, what's the matter with kids today?"

I thought I was done with the issue. *Phi Delta Kappan* editor the late Pauline Gough thought so too. She said, "I guess they can't say nasty things about schools anymore." We did not yet realize that the people saying nasty things not only didn't really *care* what the data said but were trying to hide the truth about the condition of American schools.

More data came my way. In February 1992, a new international study in mathematics and science was published and spun to emphasize the worst. In April, I went to Gough and suggested a follow-up. She said fine. I sent in a document with the title "The True Crisis in American Public Education" and a Post-It note on page 1 saying, "I'm not happy with this title, but I can't think of anything better. You guys come up with something zippy." The editors' zippy title was "The Second Bracey Report on the

Condition of Public Education," and they wanted it to be a periodic, if not necessarily annual, event.[29]

What I had seen as a single article, created by the accident of reading Cohen's column, had now come to occupy pretty much the waking hours of my life. I gave workshops and speeches and wrote more articles. I got called a contrarian (American Association of School Administrators), a messenger of complacency (Diane Ravitch), Chicken Little in Reverse (consultant Denis Doyle), and the Diogenes of Data (James Cizek, president of Audio Education). In 2003, Chester E. (Checker) Finn Jr. pronounced me "beneath contempt."[30] My, my, with enemies like Checker . . .

The points of this story are two. The first you already know: life is uncertain and will take you down unanticipated alleys and byways that might lead to dead ends or superhighways. The second is that I did not set out for some personal, political, or ideological reason to defend public schools. And certainly not for financial gain. I started

> *I started collecting data and eventually the data* compelled *the conclusion that* A Nation at Risk *was a lie.*

collecting data and eventually the data *compelled* the conclusion that *A Nation at Risk* was a lie. Nothing since that first article in 1991 has caused me to change any conclusion reached save for one:

I started by writing about American schools, but "American schools" is a fiction. One article I wrote that no one saw fit to publish was titled "First World, Third World, All Right Here at Home." Among the data therein were those showing that of the forty-one nations in the Third International Mathematics and Science Study (TIMSS), only six topped the highest-scoring U.S. states in math and only one outscored them in science. For the lowest-scoring states, though, only three of the forty-one nations scored lower.

The range of scores among different groups in this country is extraordinary, something highlighted in the chapter on international comparisons. The fact remains, though, as the draft but not the published version of the Sandia report concluded: "There are many serious problems in American public education, but there is no systemwide crisis." And so, I am able to experience the warmth that comes from giving speeches that tell people what I know they want to hear while holding firmly at the same time that I am telling them the truth.

Notes

1. Haney, Walt, and Anastasia Raczek. 1994. "Surmounting Outcomes Accountability in Education." Paper prepared for the Office of Technology Assessment. Available from the senior author at the School of Education, Boston College, Chestnut Hill, Massachusetts.

2. Gallup Organization. 2003. "Military, Police Top Gallup's Annual Confidence in Institutions Poll." Princeton, NJ: Gallup Organization, September.

3. Rickover, Hyman. 1959. *Education and Freedom.* New York: E. P. Dutton.

4. Bestor, Arthur. 1953. *Educational Wastelands: The Retreat from Learning in Our Public Schools.* Champaign, IL: University of Illinois Press.

5. Kozol, Jonathan. 1967. *Death at an Early Age.* New York: New American Library.

6. Silberman, Charles. 1970. *Crisis in the Classroom.* New York: Random House.

7. National Commission on Excellence in Education. 1983. *A Nation at Risk.* Washington, DC: National Commission on Excellence in Education.

8. Holton, Gerald. 2003. "An Insider's View of *A Nation at Risk* and Why It Still Matters." *Chronicle of Higher Education* (25 April).

9. Koret Task Force. 2003. *Our Schools and Our Future . . . Are We Still at Risk?* Palo Alto, CA: Koret Task Force.

10. Du Pont, Pete. 2003. "Two Decades of Mediocrity." *Wall Street Journal,* 5 May.

11. Harvey, James. 2003. "Nation's Students Still at Risk." *Seattle Times,* 4 May.

12. Bracey, Gerald W. 2003. "April Foolishness: The Twentieth Anniversary of *A Nation at Risk.*" *Phi Delta Kappan* (April): 616–21.

13. In his retrospective on *Risk's* twentieth anniversary, Ted Sizer pointed to an earlier, more important report, *Youth: Transition to Adulthood.* In Sizer's opinion, this report gathered dust on shelves largely because it was *not* cast in colorful terms, but rather in the scholarly prose of its senior author, James S. Coleman. Sizer, Ted. 2003. "A Nation at Risk: The Next Generation." *Education Week* (23 April). Coleman, James S., Robert H. Bremner, Burton R. Clark, et al. 1974. *Youth: Transition to Adulthood.* Chicago: University of Chicago Press.

14. Harwood, Richard. 1994. "Reporting On, By, and For an Elite." *Washington Post*, 28 May, 29.

15. O'Neill, Barry. 1994. "Anatomy of a Hoax." *New York Times Magazine*, 6 March, 46–49.

16. Raspberry, William. 1994. "The Secret of How-To Know How." *Washington Post*, 19 December, A27.

17. Daggett, Willard. 1994. "Today's Kids, Yesterday's Schooling." *Executive Education* (June): 18–21.

18. Manning, Anita. 1992. "U.S. Kids Near Top of Class in Reading." *USA Today*, 29 September, A1.

19. Archibald, George. 2003. "U.S. Fourth-Graders Rank Ninth Overall in Reading Survey." *Washington Times*, 9 April.

20. Tench, Megan. 2003. "U.S. Fares Well in World Reading Test." *Boston Globe*, 9 April.

21. Rothstein, Kevin. 2003. "U.S. Kids Rank Ninth in International Reading Study." *Boston Herald*, 9 April.

22. Cohen, Richard. 1990. "Johnny's Miserable SAT's." *Washington Post*, 4 September, A19.

23. Angoff, William H. 1971. *The College Board Admissions Testing Program: A Technical Report*. New York: College Entrance Examination Board. The 41 percent figure appeared in "S.A.T. as Democratizer," a letter to the editor of the *New York Times* by then Board President Donald Stewart, 8 May 1998, p. A22.

24. Bracey, Gerald W. 1990. "SAT Scores: Miserable or Miraculous?" *Education Week* (21 November).

25. Miller, Julie. 1991. "Report Questioning 'Crisis' in Education Triggers an Uproar." *Education Week* (13 November).

26. Carson, C. C., R. M. Huelskamp, and T. D. Woodall. 1993. "Perspectives on Education in America." *Journal of Educational Research* (May/June): 149–210.

27. Educational Testing Service (ETS). 1991. *Performance at the Top: From Elementary Through Graduate School*. Princeton, NJ: ETS.

28. Bracey, Gerald W. 1991. "Why Can't They Be Like We Were?" *Phi Delta Kappan* (October): 104–17.

29. Bracey, Gerald W. 1992. "The Second Bracey Report on the Condition of Public Education." *Phi Delta Kappan* (October): 104–17.

30. Hardy, Larry. 2003. "The Contrarian." *American School Board Journal* (October): 19–23.

More Years in School = Dumber Kids?

How can I respond when people say, "In America today, the longer you stay in school, the dumber you get relative to your peers in other industrialized nations"?

You can say, "Performance does appear to tail off a bit between grades 4 and 8 but not between grades 8 and 12."

Former Secretary of Education William J. Bennett uttered precisely the "dumber you get" statement in a speech at the Heritage Foundation.[1] The document describing the No Child Left Behind program repeats this claim, although in not quite so crass language. And, in his penultimate State of the Union speech, so did Bill Clinton.[2] It is cliché and a mantra. It's not true. Or, more precisely, it's sorta half true and we should think about the conditions that make it half true. They constitute a cause for concern, but hardly a crisis.

The cliché originates in three reports on the Third International Mathematics and Science Study, conducted in 1995. Among twenty-six nations, American fourth graders scored above average in mathematics and near the top in science. Among forty-one nations, American eighth graders rated average in both subjects. And among a varying number of countries (depending on the test), American high school seniors, apparently, dropped to near the bottom.

The operative word in the last sentence, though, is *apparently*. One can utter the cliché only if one uncritically accepts the TIMSS Final Year of Secondary School results, something one should not do. (TIMSS officials carefully used the term *final year* because the

final year of secondary school in many countries does not corre-
spond to the senior year in an American high school, nor are
those final years comparable across the other countries. At the

Rank	Country	Percent Correct
1.5	Korea	76
1.5	Singapore	76
3	Japan	74
4	Hong Kong	73
5	Netherlands	69
6	Czech Republic	66
7	Austria	65
8.5	Slovenia	64
8.5	Hungary	64
11	Ireland	63
11	United States	63
11	Australia	63
13	Canada	60
14.5	Israel	59
14.5	Latvia	59
16	Scotland	58
17	England	57
18	Cyprus	54
19.5	Norway	53
19.5	New Zealand	53
21	Greece	51
22.5	Iceland	50
22.5	Thailand	50
24	Portugal	48
25	Iran	38
26	Kuwait	32

Note: Where countries have the same score, convention calls for
them to have the average of the ranks involved. Thus, Slovenia and
Hungary, both with a score of 64, receive a rank of 8.5, the average
of 8 and 9. Similarly, Ireland, the U.S., and Australia all receive a
rank of 11, the average of 10, 11, and 12.

Source: Mathematics Achievement in the Primary School Years. 1997.
Boston College, Chestnut Hill, Massachusetts.

Figure 1–1. TIMSS Fourth-Grade Math Results

Rank	Country	Percent Correct
1	Korea	74
2	Japan	70
3	Netherlands	67
5	United States	66
5	Australia	66
5	Austria	66
7.5	Czech Republic	65
7.5	Singapore	65
9.5	Canada	64
9.5	Slovenia	64
11	England	63
12.5	Hong Kong	62
12.5	Hungary	62
14	Ireland	61
16	Norway	60
16	New Zealand	60
16	Scotland	60
18	Israel	57
19	Latvia	56
20	Iceland	55
21	Greece	54
22	Cyprus	51
23	Portugal	50
24	Thailand	49
25	Iran	40
26	Kuwait	39

Source: *Science Achievement in the Primary School Years*. Boston College, Chestnut Hill, Massachusetts.

Figure 1–2. TIMSS Fourth-Grade Science Results

press conference attending the release of the study in this country, however, the U.S. Department of Education made it seem as though the study compared twelfth graders in this country to twelfth graders elsewhere.)

The fourth-grade and eighth-grade results are relatively straightforward. These results, in terms of percent correct, are given in Figures 1–1, 1–2, 1–3, and 1–4.

Why should the performance of American students decline

Rank	Country	Percent Correct
1	SINGAPORE	79
2	Japan	73
3	Korea	72
4	Hong Kong	70
5.5	Belgium (Flemish)	66
5.5	Czech Republic	66
8.5	Slovak Republic	62
8.5	Switzerland	62
8.5	Hungary	62
8.5	Austria	62
11.5	France	61
11.5	Slovenia	61
14	Russian Federation	60
14	Bulgaria	60
14	Netherlands	60
17	Canada	59
17	Ireland	59
17	Belgium (French)	59
20	Australia	58
21.5	Thailand	57
21.5	Israel	57
23	Sweden	56
25	England	54
25	Norway	54
25	Germany	54
27.5	UNITED STATES	53
27.5	New Zealand	53
29.5	Scotland	52
29.5	Denmark	52
31.5	Latvia	51
31.5	Spain	51
33	Iceland	50
34.5	Greece	49
34.5	Romania	49
36.5	Lithuania	48
36.5	Cyprus	48
38	Portugal	43
39	Iran	38
40	Colombia	29
41	SOUTH AFRICA	24

INTERNATIONAL AVERAGE = 55

Source: Mathematics Achievement in the Middle School Years. 1996. Boston College, Chestnut Hill, Massachusetts.

Figure 1–3. TIMSS Middle School Math Results (1996)

Rank	Country	Percent Correct
1	SINGAPORE	70
2	Korea	66
3	Japan	65
4	Czech Republic	64
6	Bulgaria	62
6	Netherlands	62
6	Slovenia	62
9	England	61
9	Hungary	61
9	Austria	61
11.5	Belgium (Flemish)	60
11.5	Australia	60
14	Slovak Republic	59
14	Sweden	59
14	Canada	59
19	Ireland	58
19	UNITED STATES	58
19	Russian Federation	58
19	New Zealand	58
19	Norway	58
19	Hong Kong	58
19	Germany	58
23.5	Thailand	57
23.5	Israel	57
25.5	Switzerland	56
25.5	Spain	56
27	Scotland	55
28	France	54
29.5	Greece	52
29.5	Iceland	52
31	Denmark	51
33.5	Latvia	50
33.5	Portugal	50
33.5	Belgium (French)	50
33.5	Romania	50
36	Lithuania	49
37.5	Iran	47
37.5	Cyprus	47
39	Kuwait	43
40	Colombia	39
41	SOUTH AFRICA	27

INTERNATIONAL AVERAGE = 56

Source: Science Achievement in the Middle School Years. 1996. Boston College, Chestnut Hill, Massachusetts.

Figure 1–4. TIMSS Middle School Science Results (1996)

relative to their peers abroad between fourth grade and eighth grade? Two reasons offer themselves as explanations and neither leads to the conclusion that the kids are getting dumber.

First, American kids lug around textbooks that are about three times as thick as those in other nations. Many math and science textbooks abroad generally contain 110 to 150 pages. In recent years, many cartoons have turned on how children cannot stand up under the textbook loads on their backs. Serious articles have discussed the burden children carry around. Their weight causes pediatricians to sound alarms about the increased incidence of scoliosis and other serious spinal diseases that these heavy loads can bring on.[3, 4]

In most countries, the state directs the production of textbooks and controls the content. In America, private, for-profit companies, mostly the publishing houses of huge conglomerates, produce the textbooks. These corporations want to sell to the widest possible markets (while being extra sensitive to appease those two populous states with statewide textbook adoptions, California and Texas). They thus take a kitchen-sink approach to the books, stuffing them with every option a state might want.[5] American teachers try to cover it all. As a consequence, teachers "cover" too many topics too fast. Understanding suffers. The material must be reviewed the next year because it didn't take. A TIMSS study found that European and Asian teachers spend much more time on many fewer topics. In addition, the TIMSS video study found American teachers, at least in math, emphasizing algorithms and procedures rather than understanding.

Second, American educators have traditionally regarded the middle school years as a time for review and consolidation (maybe as a result of the previous reason). Those years prepare students for the more intense study of high school. In many other countries, the middle years actually start that intense secondary school study. Thus, Japanese students receive considerable instruction in algebra in the seventh grade and plane geometry in the eighth, while most American students bump up against these subjects as courses in ninth and tenth grade, respectively.

Related to the middle-years-as-review practice is the belief held by a number of middle school teachers and specialists that these years should *not* be a time of intense intellectual work, but rather one of attention to emerging sexuality and the search for identity. Linda Perlstein's *Not Much, Just Chillin'* provides a graphic, if chilling (no pun intended), look at this period of children's lives. Interviewed on National Public Radio's *All Things Considered,* Perlstein said, "Parents can be thankful that middle school ends."[6]

The European and Asian approach might well be as much a historical artifact as a reasoned pedagogy. Until recently, many nations had high dropout rates in high school. For instance, in 1985's Second International Mathematics Study, while 100 percent of Hungarian seniors still studied math, only 50 percent of age-eligible students were even in school. Currently, some European countries have higher high school graduation rates than the United States. Historically, though, if these nations felt everyone needed to study a particular subject, they had to get it into the curriculum by eighth grade.

You might not have much luck getting people to listen to your explanation of why American students do not fall farther behind between grade 8 and grade 12 because the reasons are multiple and some are a little technical. They are valid reasons nonetheless. In sum, you can say that the TIMSS final year study did not compare apples to apples or even apples to oranges. It was more like apples to aardvarks. In addition, in one

TIMSS final year study did not compare apples to apples or even apples to oranges.

of the tests, advanced mathematics, the American contingent used a sample that had not studied a lot of what was on the test. Kids don't test well on things they haven't studied. Really.

After eighth grade, most American students go on to comprehensive high schools. After eighth grade, Europe and Asia sort students into differentiated curricula in different schools (in Germany, the selection starts at fourth grade, although this procedure has recently come in for heavy criticism). In some countries, more than 50 percent of the students enter vocational programs. Others head for an arts and humanities program or a science and technology program. These programs might or might not culminate in admission to college. Thus, in a number of the countries, the students tested in the final year study had had quite different secondary school experiences than their American "counterparts."

In the final year study, nations were supposed to administer a general "math/science literacy" test to a national probability sample—not all countries did. Nations chose the students they felt most appropriate to test physics and advanced mathematics, the other two tests administered. Allowing countries to choose was appropriate because we wouldn't get an accurate picture of what final year students knew if we tested students in advanced mathematics who had not gone beyond, say, plane geometry or assessed students in physics who had not studied that natural science at all. But allowing choice only served to increase the differences among the samples.

For instance, Sweden and Norway topped other countries in physics. And why not? They tested students who had taken three years of physics. American students usually take only one year if they take any at all. A few might take a second year, usually the Advanced Placement course from the College Board or some local honors course.

Should American high schools offer more multiyear programs in physics and other natural sciences? That is a legitimate question. It is difficult to imagine where the nation would find the necessary cadre of qualified teachers—or the money to pay them—but it is still a legitimate question. It is *not* legitimate to compare students who have studied a subject for one year with those who have studied it for three.

In the case of the advanced mathematics test, the selection of the American sample guaranteed a poor showing. The U.S. sample consisted of students who had taken calculus and those who had taken a precalculus course. When I asked TIMSS officials why we had included the precalculus kids, I received a quite casual answer: "Oh, just to see how they'd do." Well, they did awful. They scored one hundred points below American students who actually had calculus under their belts. To get an idea of what a hundred-point difference means, assume that American students who had taken calculus scored at the fiftieth percentile (which, in fact, they did). The students from precalculus classes, then, scored at the sixteenth percentile.

Understanding why the two groups performed differently presents no great mystery: 23 percent of the items on the advanced mathematics test *presumed* that the students had actually taken calculus. As noted earlier, when tested on what they haven't studied, students don't do well. It would be one thing if the results were just used "to see how they'd do," but no one told the media about the precalculus kids in the sample and the media used the results to pound American students and American schools. If the analysis had been limited to those who had taken calculus—the group of American students most like the European sample—the United States would have finished with an average rank, the same position occupied by eighth graders.

To understand the problems with the math/science literacy results, we have to back up and take note of some cultural characteristics here and abroad. Most nations do not have the culture of public self-criticism found in the United States. Indeed, in some countries, criticizing the government can get you locked up, tortured, or executed. A man with dual American-Egyptian citizenship is currently serving eight years in an Egyptian jail. His crime? He criticized Egyptian President Mubarak for not preparing a successor.

The United States has consistently drawn national probability samples for international studies (the procedure it follows for NAEP). Left to their own designs, though, many nations would choose to test students who would make the country look good. To counter this tendency, TIMSS officials hired Statistics Canada in Ottawa to draw the samples for all nations. Statistics Canada specializes in drawing samples. All participating nations provided StatCan, as it's called, with a list of all schools in the nation and some demographic characteristics of each. StatCan then drew the samples. TIMSS staff established criteria for whether or not a nation met the sampling design and the participation rate needed for valid data.

Of course, in some nations, one cannot force a selected school to take part, and at all ages, some countries failed to meet the sampling and participation rate criteria. At grades 4 and 8, even if we eliminated such countries, we would still have a large array of nations. Not in the final year study, however. We have observed that nations could choose whom to test in advanced mathematics and in physics. For the math/science literacy test, though, they were supposed to use the samples drawn by Statistics Canada. Only eight of the twenty-one participating countries met the criteria for valid data. What kind of a study is that? The TIMSS final year study contains so many methodological flaws that I don't think the Honors Committee at William and Mary would have accepted it had I offered it as an honors thesis. Had I turned it in to the psychology department at Stanford as a doctoral thesis, I would have been laughed across the bay to Berkeley and told to major in sociology or something.

Those of us who have lived abroad will never fully trust international comparisons because of the mostly impossible to quantify cultural differences. For example, I have friends with grandchildren in French schools. They throw up their hands in horror at how French teachers use shame as a motivational tool. A teacher might put the worst paper from an assignment on the bulletin board and make fun of it. What does this do to or for educational outcomes? Is the humiliation French children endure in school responsible for their prowess at repartee as adults? Do the kids sit there formulating in their heads clever, retaliatory bon mots that they would say if they dared? Who knows?

The TIMSS final year study did manage to quantify one cultural variable: the number of hours worked at a paid job. In most developed nations, you are a student or a worker, not both (except in other Anglophone countries; this might be a legacy of British mercantilism, which justified the exploitation of child labor). And once you stop being a student, you can't restart. Europeans are amazed at what they call the "second chance" aspect of American education.

Research in this nation on the relationship between work and school performance is relatively (but not completely) consistent: students who work up to twenty hours a week do better in school than those who work longer hours or who don't work at all. When social class is taken into account (poor students are more likely to have to work to support family, middle-class students to support their car, date, movie, and concert habits), most interpretations attribute the improvement to a sense of responsibility—the people at the job site count on me—and learning to manage time. After twenty hours, though, work time interferes with meals and sleep and school.

This curvilinear relationship between hours worked at a job and academic performance shows up in TIMSS. The table in Figure 1–5 presents the results for American students and for a more typical nation, Sweden. It shows the percentage of students working a given number of hours at a paid job and their scores on the math/science literacy test.

Thus, under the column "1–7 hours" we find that 39 percent

Effect of Hours Worked at a Paying Job on TIMSS Final Year Study

Hours Worked Per Week

	1–7 hours	7–14 hours	21–35 hours	35+ hours
Percent of Students (Average Score)				
United States	39 (484)	7 (506)	27 (474)	28 (448)
Sweden	84 (563)	9 (541)	5 (511)	3 (497)

International Average = 500

Source: Mathematics and Science Achievement in the Final Year of Secondary School. 1998. Boston College, Chestnut Hill, Massachusetts.

Figure 1–5. Effect of Hours Worked at a Paying Job on TIMSS Final Year Study

of American students who worked between one and seven hours per week obtained an average score of 484. Eighty-four percent of Swedish students who worked the same number of hours received an average score of 563.

The figure that jumps out from this table is that 55 percent of American seniors reported working more hours at a paid job than is good for them. Twenty-seven percent worked twenty-one to thirty-five hours a week and 28 percent worked more than thirty-five hours a week. It shows in their scores, 474 and 488, respectively.

Once again, when we parse through the group of Americans who took the tests to find students most similar to those in other nations, American students land in the middle of the pack, just as they did at eighth grade.

Finally, in regard to TIMSS, I am unaware of any researcher who has studied the "senior slump" phenomenon across countries. Certainly it does not likely occur for those students in England, France, or Germany who are gearing up to take their important tests, the A-Levels, *Baccalaureat,* and *Abitur,* respectively. Or in Japan, with its period of "examination hell," the senior year, or in South Korea, where the college entrance exam frenzy makes stressed-out Japan look relaxed.[7]

One would expect students in any nation with a series of final-year national tests at the senior level to be focused. Here, of course, seniors pretty much have a sense of what their future looks like in the years immediately following twelfth grade, and they slack off. Thus I wonder how much the senior slump depressed the final year scores. TIMSS tests meant nothing to the students—they received no rewards, punishments, or even feedback on how they had done—but in order to get as close to the end of the final year as possible, the tests were administered in May.

The results from PISA, the Program of International Student Assessment, also counter contentions that American student performance declines in high school relative to that of students in other developed nations. PISA was organized and administered through the Organized for Economic Cooperation and Development, headquartered in Paris.

PISA had a different purpose than TIMSS. TIMSS looked at how well students had mastered what they had been taught in school. PISA sought to assess how well they could apply what they knew to new situations. Many of the PISA items are too complex to be summarized easily, but here is one that illustrates what the test was trying to measure.

The item presents the student with a map of Antarctica. On the map is a legend for distance. The student's task is to estimate the area of the continent. You might want to take a minute to think about how to solve this problem. At least two solution strategies are available. You can draw a rectangle around the continent, use the distance legend to measure the lengths of two sides of the rectangle, and then calculate the area by multiplying the lengths of the two sides. Similarly, and more accurately given Antarctica's shape, you can draw a circle around the continent, use the legend for distance to calculate the length of the radius of the circle, and solve for area.

Thus, to answer this problem, you need to know something you learned in school, the formulas for the area of a rectangle and a circle, but you must also be able to see how those formulas can be applied to a problem where it is not immediately obvious that they are required.

PISA tested fifteen-year-olds, which would mean mostly tenth graders in this country. Thirty-two nations participated. American tenth graders in PISA looked much like American eighth graders in TIMSS: they finished smack in the middle on all three subjects tested. Among the nations tested, American students finished fifteenth in reading, nineteenth in mathematics, and fourteenth in science. They scored four points above, seven points below, and one point below the international averages, respectively.

Most countries scored quite close together. Only three of the thirty-two countries had significantly higher scores in reading than the U.S., while eight had significantly higher scores in mathematics, and seven had significantly higher scores in science. The "significance" involved here, of course, is statistical significance, not practical significance. Only one of the statistically significantly higher countries, Finland, also outscores the U.S. in some years on measures of global competitiveness produced by the World Economic Forum.

The Meaning of Statistical Significance

In a number of places in this book, the reader will encounter the phrase *statistical significance* or *statistically significant*. These are important research terms. They are technical terms, but they can be explained in plain English.

Statistical significance is a statement about odds. Suppose you look at the reading test scores of two groups of students taught to read with different approaches, say, phonics and whole language. Let's say one group got thirty-two out of forty items correct and the other got twenty-seven correct. A test of statistical significance will tell you how likely it is (a statement about odds) that these two groups really differ. Or, as statisticians say, how likely is it that the two groups really came from populations with the same mean?

To rephrase a bit, tests of statistical significance tell you how likely it is that a difference as large as the five-point difference you found (between thirty-two and twenty-seven) occurred by chance. If the result is not likely to have occurred by chance, the result is termed statistically significant.

You might well ask why we need such tests. After all, you found a five-point difference. Isn't that real? Maybe, maybe not. We need statistical tests because we don't test populations. If we tested populations, then any differences we found would be real (assuming tests with no measurement error), but we'd have to administer about four million tests for each grade we were interested in. That would be prohibitively expensive. So we test samples. We often test "samples of convenience," namely, the kids in the nearby schools.

Because we test samples, we can't be completely sure that our results are precisely what we would obtain if we did test populations. If we tested two other samples of children with the reading test, we might not see any differences at all or we might see larger or smaller differences. The differences among different samples is called *sampling error* and the tests of significance take sampling error into account.

Researchers can be heard saying things like "significant at the point oh five level" and "pea less than point oh one." As written numbers, "point oh five" and "point oh one" look like this: .05 and .01. "Pea" is the letter *p*, which in stat talk stands for probability. To say something is significant at the .05 level is to say that the chances are less than one in twenty (or that the probability is less than one in twenty) that the results we observed happened by chance. The .01 level means that the chance occurrence has been reduced to less than one in a hundred.

For the record, here are the actual scores of selected nations:

Rank	Reading	Mathematics	Science
1.	Finland, 546	Japan, 557	South Korea, 552
5.	Ireland, 527	Australia, 533	Canada, 529
10.	Austria, 507	France, 517	Sweden, 512
15.	United States, 504	Ireland, 503	Hungary, 496
20.	Italy, 487	Germany, 490	Germany, 487
25.	Poland, 479	Russian Federation, 478	Liechtenstein, 476
30.	Luxembourg, 441	Luxembourg, 446	Luxembourg, 443

The U.S. Department of Education's report on PISA contained a disturbing but informative set of statistics: scores for the three largest ethnic groups—blacks, whites, and Hispanics. The report omitted Asians because in a study like PISA, too few of them would be sampled to provide a reliable separate group estimate.

Suppose the entire sample of American students were made up of only black or only white or only Hispanic students. If we took the scores of each ethnic group and held them up to the scores of other nations, how would they rank? Here is the answer:

	Reading	Math	Science
White Students	2nd	7th	4th
Black Students	29th	30th	30th
Hispanic Students	29th	30th	30th

Thus, if white students constituted a nation, it would rank second in the world in reading and near the top on all three subjects, while black and Hispanic students would fall near the bottom. The reasons this should be so are multifold. First, about 40 percent of all black and Hispanic students live in poverty, and poverty depresses achievement (see Chapter 3 for proof of this contention). Second, many Hispanics do not speak English as their native language. Many of those can no doubt navigate conversations in English and even classwork, but tests present more subtle text.

People's opinions differ greatly on why black students score low. The late anthropologist John Ogbu and his colleague Astrid Davis as well as linguist John McWhorter have argued that cultural factors play a large role.[8,] [9,] [10] So do Abigail and Stephan Thernstrom in *No Excuses: Closing the Racial Gap in Learning*[11] and *New York Times* columnist Bob Herbert.[12] In particular, the popular notion that doing well in school is "acting white" and to be avoided at all costs depresses black achievement. "I have no idea what the stats are," says Herbert, "but I know this perverse peer pressure to do less than your best in scholarly and intellectual pursuits is holding back large numbers of black Americans, especially black boys and men."

On the other hand, the National Urban League's Ronald Ross, described by *Washington Post* columnist William Raspberry as a "militant black educator," echoes George W. Bush's charge about the "soft bigotry of low expectations." He claims white teachers and administrators don't have high expectations for black kids. Raspberry appears to challenge Ross, pointing out that in the

> *In particular, the popular notion that doing well in school is "acting white" and to be avoided at all costs depresses black achievement.*

District of Columbia, the overwhelming majority of teachers and administrators are black, yet low achievement prevails.[13]

In *Schools and Class: Using Social, Economic, and Educational Reform to Close the Black-White Achievement Gap,* Richard Rothstein points to the essential silliness of trying to close the gap using only educational reform and the schools:

> Although conventional opinion is that "failing" schools contribute mightily to the achievement gap, evidence indicates that schools already do a great deal to combat it. Most of the social class difference in average academic potential exists by the time children are three years old. This difference is exacerbated during the years that children spend in school, but during these years, the growth in the gap occurs mostly in after-school hours and during the summertime, when children are not actually in classrooms. (11)[14]

As indicated by the title, social and economic reforms must occur as well. The book describes what some of these reforms might look like.

Whatever the reasons and the causes, it is clear that the United States doesn't need a program like No Child Left Behind. That program claims we must test every kid every year to find out who is indeed being left behind. We already know where the problems are. We know where the resources are needed. We have lacked the political will to act on our knowledge.

> *We already know where the problems are. We know where the resources are needed. We have lacked the political will to act on our knowledge*

Why do people make such a fuss about how various countries score on tests? People took our supposed last-place finish in the TIMSS final year study as a major blow and PISA did for Germany what *A Nation at Risk* had done for us—not only did it garner German schools a lot of negative publicity, but it sent Germans in droves looking for answers in another country (Finland) (see my November 2002 Research column in *Phi Delta Kappan* for a full discussion of PISA and its impact on Germany). People fuss about international test score rankings because for about twenty years, people assumed, and some people still assume, that test scores influence a country's ability to compete in the global marketplace. Particularly in the 1980s, critics bashed schools for forfeiting our top rank in competitiveness. Japan had high test scores and was enjoying an "economic miracle." People leapt to an inappropriate, illogical conclusion: Japan's high-scoring students are responsible for its becoming a mighty economic power. I address this misconception in Chapter 2.

The Limits of Tests

This chapter has dealt with the "success" or "failure" of educational systems as defined by test scores. Other chapters will also make or refute arguments by using test scores. Tests have become the common currency of comparison in international studies and, all too often, the sole criterion when evaluating schools domestically. This is most unfortunate because tests don't work very well for this purpose. Tests scores are correlated with socioeconomic status and often don't generalize beyond themselves. That is, if a second test is brought in to corroborate the scores on a first test, the scores on the second test are lower than on the first: the achievement seems somewhat limited to the specific questions of the first test. The current crop of tests also falls short because they do not provide teachers or administrators with any information about what to do next. As Robert Mislevy put it, "It is only a slight exaggeration to describe the test theory that dominates educational measurement today as the application of twentieth century statistics to nineteenth century psychology."[15]

More important are the things that tests don't or can't measure. Some years ago, in a critique of proposed changes in the National Assessment of Educational Progress, the National Academy of Education put the problem thusly:

> Many of those personal qualities that we hold dear—resilience and courage in the face of stress, a sense of craft in our work, a commitment to justice and caring in our social relationships, a dedication to advancing the public good in communal life—are exceedingly difficult to assess. And so, unfortunately, we are apt to measure what we can, and eventually come to value what is measured over what is left unmeasured. The shift is subtle and occurs gradually.[16]

The Academy wrote that in 1987. That was then, this is now. The shift has occurred and there is nothing subtle about it anymore. Testing is a juggernaut. E. L. Thorndike's credo of 1918 has been reversed. Thorndike held, "Whatever exists at all exists in some amount."[17] Therefore, it can be measured. Today people act more like "If it isn't measured, it doesn't exist."

But, looking at the NAE passage one day, I composed a list, hardly exhaustive, of qualities that we either don't use tests to measure or qualities that tests cannot measure. My list looks like this:

creativity	self-discipline
critical thinking	leadership
resilience	civic-mindedness
motivation	courage
persistence	cowardice
curiosity	compassion
endurance	resourcefulness
reliability	sense of beauty
enthusiasm	sense of wonder
empathy	honesty
self-awareness	integrity

Hard to measure, these qualities, but are they not what really count in life? The story of abuses in the Abu Ghraib prison in Iraq brought to mind the experiments of Stanley Milgram in the 1960s. In Milgram's experiment, replicated all over the world, people were instructed to administer shocks to another person strapped into a chair with electrodes on. These people were told they were part of an experiment on the effect of punishment on learning.

No shocks were actually delivered. The person in the chair was a stooge—a trained actor paid the play the role. The machine to deliver the shocks was scaled from 15 to 450 volts and the person to administer the shocks was actually given a 45-volt shock to experience what it felt like.

When the shock reached 75 volts, the man in the chair grunted; at 120 volts, he complained loudly; at 150 volts he demanded to be released from the experiment; his protests became more vehement and emotional until at 285 volts he emitted only an agonized scream. Soon thereafter, he made no sounds at all.

Yet, at the insistence of a white-coated experimenter whom the person giving the shocks had never met before, 60 percent of the people in the experiment were willing to go all the way to 450 volts.

How did these 60 percent differ from the other 40 who refused and stopped the experiment? On their test scores? Somehow, I doubt that test scores played much of a role.

Of course, a teacher cannot teach these qualities the way she can arithmetic. She can model them, or talk about other people who are exemplars of one or more of them. But not if she has to get the kids ready to pass a test.

Tests need to be kept in perspective and right now in America, the proper perspective has been largely lost.

Notes

1. Bennett, William J. 2000. "The State, and Future of American Education." Speech to the Heritage Foundation, March. No longer available at the Heritage Foundation website.

2. Clinton, William J. 1999. State of the Union Address, January.

3. Maraghy, Mary. 1999. "Loaded Up for Learning." *Florida Times-Union,* 16 December, A1.

4. Oshrant, Carmiel. 2000. "Parents and Doctors Say the Load Students Are Carrying Is Too Heavy." *Philadelphia Inquirer,* 21 May, A1.

5. Bismarck said one shouldn't look at sausages or legislation as it is being made. Harriet Tyson-Bernstein's *A Conspiracy of Good Intentions: America's Textbook Fiasco* (Washington, DC: Council for Basic Education, 1988) adds a third item to Bismarck's list.

6. Perlstein, Linda. 2003. *Not Much, Just Chillin': The Hidden Lives of Middle Schoolers.* New York: Farrar, Strauss & Giroux.

7. A seldom-noted outcome of this procedure is that once admitted to a prestigious college, Japanese and Korean students enter a period of prolonged intellectual hibernation. On opening night of an assessment class I teach at George Mason University, I had students introduce themselves and say why they were taking the course. One student was from South Korea and had a bachelor's degree from one of the three

high-prestige universities in the nation (they have a collective acceptance rate of 1.7 percent). She said she was reentering university "to actually study something."

8. Ogbu, John, and Astrid Davis. 2003. *Black American Students in an Affluent Suburb: A Study of Academic Disadvantage.* Mahwah, NJ: Lawrence Erlbaum.

9. John McWhorter. 2000. *Losing the Race: Self Sabotage in Black America.* New York: Free Press.

10. McWhorter, John. 2003. "How Hip-hop Holds Blacks Back." *City Journal* (summer).

11. Thernstrom, Abigail, and Stephan Thernstrom. 2003. *No Excuses: Closing the Racial Gap in Learning.* New York: Simon and Schuster.

12. Herbert, Bob. 2003. "Breaking Away." *New York Times,* 11 July, A23.

13. Raspberry, William. 2002. "Why Black Kids Lag." *Washington Post,* 9 December, A23.

14. Rothstein, Richard. 2004. *Schools and Class: Using Social, Economic, and Educational Reform to Close the Black-White Achievement Gap.* Washington, DC: Economic Policy Institute.

15. Mislevy, Robert J. 1993. "Foundations of a New Test Theory." In *Test Theory for a New Generation of Tests,* ed. Norman J. Frederiksen. Princeton, NJ: Educational Testing Service.

16. Alexander, Lamar, and H. Thomas James. 1987. *The Nation's Report Card: Improving the Assessment of Student Achievement.* Cambridge, MA: National Academy of Education.

17. Thorndike, Edward L. 1918. "The Nature, Purposes and General Methods of Measurements of Educational Products." In *Seventeenth NSSE Yearbook.* Bloomington, IL: National Society for the Study of Education.

Lousy Schools = Lousy Workforce?

What do I say when people say lousy schools are producing a lousy workforce and that is killing us in the global marketplace?

You can say that the American worker, the most productive in the world, is getting more so.[1] You can say that in its Global Competitiveness Report 2002–2003, the World Economic Forum (WEF), a high-profile think tank in Geneva, ranks the United States number one among eighty countries in overall competitiveness, number one in growth competitiveness, and number one in microeconomic competitiveness.[2] Finally, you can point out that test scores don't have much to do with how competitive a country is.[3]

The publication of *A Nation at Risk* in 1983 made explicit the widely held, but implicit link between test scores and economic health and global competitiveness. America was in bad shape. President Jimmy Carter had taken a lot of guff in the late 1970s for saying that the country suffered from "malaise." But the prime rate had soared above 20 percent (at the time of writing, it was 4 percent), Iranians had held American soldiers as captives for more than a year, and long lines had formed at the gasoline pumps to buy what was, for Americans then, outrageously priced gas. In 1981 Ronald Reagan was president but even that perennial optimist was not yet ready to say, "It's morning again in America" (he would not say it until the presidential campaign of 1984). American cars, long known for their "planned obsolescence," fell apart with obscenely few miles registered on their odometers. Japanese and German cars ran and ran and ran. Japanese just-in-time inventory techniques offered overhead inventory savings that made it hard for American companies to compete.

Reagan's secretary of education, Terrel Bell, sought what he later called a *Sputnik*-like event that would galvanize Americans to improve their schools. Bell thought that making the country feel

Reagan's secretary of education, Terrel Bell, sought what he later called a Sputnik-like event that would galvanize Americans to improve their schools.

good about its schools was necessary to making it feel good about the rest of its institutions (really, he did). Unable to find or produce such an event, Bell settled for convening a panel he called the National Commission on Excellence in Education, even though he knew well the dust-gathering fate of most commission reports. In late April 1983, his commission delivered *A Nation at Risk*.

As noted earlier, people labeled that document, with good reason, the paper *Sputnik*. Like the real *Sputnik* in 1957, it put education in the public spotlight. Along with the Cold Warrior rhetoric cited earlier, *A Nation at Risk* made a case that our present danger was not so much that our enemies would bomb us off the planet but that our friends would outsmart us and strip us of our leadership role in the world economy. Early on, the commissioners wrote, "If only to keep and improve on the slim competitive edge we still hold in world markets, we must dedicate ourselves to the reform of our educational system" (7).[4]

The report documented the risk with statistical snippets mostly involving test scores:

- There has been a steady decline in science achievement among seventeen-year-olds, as measured by national assessments in 1969, 1971, and 1977.
- Average achievement of high school students on most standardized tests is now lower than twenty-six years ago, when *Sputnik* was launched.
- The College Board's Scholastic Aptitude Tests (SATs) demonstrate a virtually unbroken decline from 1963 to 1980.
- Average tested achievement of students graduating from college is also lower.

And on and on.

The report spun some of these statistics, selectively used some, and distorted others. Some actually did not exist.

The report spun some of these statistics, selectively used some, and distorted others. Some actually did not exist (the last one above, for example).

A Nation at Risk, though, offered no actual *evidence* that high test scores led to economic good times. The link was merely correlational: Japan, Germany, and Korea, among other nations, were enjoying economic booms and their kids scored well on tests. On the other hand, we were in the doldrums and test scores were down. In fact, the SAT bottomed out even as Bell's commission held hearings around the country, and some gave the report credit for the uptick that occurred in scores in the next couple of years, a most improbable attribution of causality.

This book provides many statistics about test scores and other quantifiable variables to show that the nation was not at risk then and isn't now. Over the years I have also accumulated experiences that bear on the "lousy schools" hypothesis but which cannot be quantified. Alfred Binet wrote in 1911 that one test means nothing, but a lot of tests mean something. These experiences, taken alone, wouldn't mean much, but taken together they add up to something significant.

As noted in Chapter 1, tests do not—cannot—measure many of the important qualities needed to enjoy life and succeed in it. Among the qualities mentioned are curiosity and creativity. While critics often accuse American schools of crushing children's creativity, they nurture it more than schools in most other countries. Consider these points:

1.   In an article in the *Washington Post* titled "At Least Our Kids Ask Questions," author Amy Biancolli recounts her travails teaching Scottish kids about Shakespeare. "It took months of badgering before I was able to get my Scottish teenagers to speak up in class. They simply weren't accustomed to asking questions or tossing around their own observations."[5] No one accuses American kids of such reticence. Indeed, at times American students are criticized for being too willing to speak without thinking their thoughts through.

Biancolli continues: "American schools teach American kids to ask questions, they teach students to be curious, skeptical, even contrary to ask for the whys and hows behind what's in the rote acquisition of facts. At their best, they teach kids to challenge the teachers." European novels are replete with the dire consequences that befall European students who dare challenge a teacher, at least openly.

2.   As a graduate student, I lived for a year in Hong Kong and after making the acquaintance of the chair of the psychology department at Hong Kong University, I occasionally lectured undergraduate students in developmental psychology. On my first outing, being a product of my culture, I did what my American professors did—I prepared lecture notes of important points to cover as well as some questions to stimulate thought and discussion. When I asked my first question, the students sat there. I stood. They sat. I stood. They sat. They won. I went on with my lecture. Afterward, I asked the chairman what had happened. He said, "Oh, they were probably embarrassed that you didn't know the answers to your questions."

In Asia, professors profess. They transfer knowledge. My tale is an old story now, but recently I recounted this tale to a professor in Taiwan and asked if it were it still true. Yes, he said. "Professors' questions are often met with stony silence." In a story about why Japanese scientists don't win Nobel prizes and Americans do, a Japanese scientist put part of the blame on the educational system. "Teachers still tell you that eloquence might be silver, but silence is golden."

Indeed, the TIMSS video study in seven nations revealed that classrooms in Japan and Hong Kong consist of nearly all teacher talk, while those in the United States and some other countries show students and teachers interacting.[6]

3.   On a trip to Japan, the educational demographer Harold Hodgkinson was approached at a soiree by a man who asked why Japanese don't win Nobels. Hodgkinson thought for a minute and then said, "To win Nobels, you have to do original research and invent things." The man wrote it down.

4.   In his 1989 book, *The Enigma of Japanese Power,* Dutch journalist Karel van Wolferen reported the tale of a Japanese scientist, Susumu Tonegawa, who did win the 1987 Nobel for medicine. Wolferen wrote that opinion in Japan was universal: Tonegawa would never have won if he had stayed in Japan.[7] Indeed, on the autobiography page of the Nobel website, Tonegawa says, "I cannot thank Professor Watanabe enough for this critical suggestion in the early phase of my career." Watanabe was Tonegawa's mentor at the University of Kyoto, where Tonegawa obtained a bachelor's degree. And what was

Watanabe's critical suggestion? Go east, young man. Specifically, go to the University of California for your Ph.D. After getting his doctorate, Tonegawa worked for a time in Switzerland, then landed a position at MIT, where he conducted his prize-winning research.

5.   In a *New York Times* article, reporter Howard French described the fate of Japanese scientist Hideki Shirakawa, who won the 2000 Nobel prize in chemistry. Shirakawa *had* conducted his research in Japan. His immediate reward for this accomplishment, aside from the prize money, was to be appointed to head a commission to increase the number of Nobels earned by Japanese scientists. The government wants at least thirty in the next fifty years. "The figure is way too high," said Shirakawa. "In the last 50 years, we've only had six." In the last decade, only Shirakawa had won for Japan. In the same ten years, forty-four American scientists claimed Nobels.[8]

Shirakawa explained the absence of prizes in terms of the Japanese tradition of being a rice culture, which requires that water must be shared by everyone and everyone must walk among the rows at the same pace. "And all of this meant that uniqueness had to be suppressed." In the harsher terms of an old Japanese adage, "The nail that stands up gets hammered down." Recall the words of another Japanese scientist earlier: "In school, teachers still teach you that eloquence might be silver, but silence is golden."

Suppressing uniqueness combined with a concern for loss of face means that Japanese lack true peer review. Peer review occurs often in American research. Researchers usually present their findings first to colleagues at the same institution and friends around the country. When the study is judged ready, they send the research to a peer-reviewed journal, which in turn sends the document to other scientists in the same field for critical, and usually anonymous, review. And I do mean *critical* review. The process is sometimes brutal as peers seek to find holes in the logic, flaws in the methodology or statistical analyses, misinterpretations of findings or other explanations for the findings than the one presented by the originator of the manuscript. Peer review involves asking question after question about the research.

French recounts one Japanese scientist saying that he worked in America for a while and often watched researchers almost come to blows while arguing over a study, then adjourn for drinks as friends. "That kind of thing happens in the United States, but, in Japan, never." French also tells the tale of an eminent climate physicist, who had returned to Japan after some years working in the United States. He planned to come back to America soon. "Many of my fellow scientists agree with me [that we need peer review], but they say I am too Americanized and complain that real peer review in Japan won't work."

6. The atmosphere around Nobel prizes is rarefied and perhaps for that reason we should not make too much of it. But American scientists disproportionately contribute to scholarly journals also, although this edge is softening as other countries catch up to the U.S.[9]

As noted earlier, the World Economic Forum ranks the United States number one in global competitiveness. There are dozens of variables that go into the WEF's overall index. The WEF labels one set of variables National Innovation Capacity. We're number one there, too. "Today," says the WEF, "competitive advantage must come from the ability to create and then commercialize new products and processes, shifting the technology frontier as fast as rivals can keep up."[10]

7. A humble coda to this section: As an elementary school student, my daughter had teachers who advised her repeatedly, "There is no such thing as a bad question." I didn't make a lot of it at the time, but think for a moment of what twelve years in a culture that values questions might do to one's thought processes and capacity for inquiry compared with one that praises silence.

The opposite of curiosity and asking questions is taking a test. If you stop to think on a test, you're in trouble. Indeed, in a section on test-wiseness in one of its SAT-preparation books, the College Board offers this advice: "Keep moving." We'd better think more than twice about replacing a culture that values questions with one that worships high test scores.

> *We'd better think more than twice about replacing a culture that values questions with one that worships high test scores.*

Innovation and creativity might not be what some people think of when they speak of a lousy workforce. They might be referring to shoddy goods or inept people on the assembly line. But even there, studies have consistently found American workers productive, often the most productive in the world using a more mundane definition of *productive:* the amount of goods produced in an hour.

Notes

1. The American advantage becomes smaller when workweek length is taken into account, and it would become smaller still if vacations were figured in.

2. The WEF contends that a nation cannot be competitive if its businesses are not competitive. The microeconomic competitive index uses 62 variables that assess the sophistication of companies and the "national business environment" in which they operate. Company variables (16) include extent of staff training, capacity for innovation, extent of branding, and company spending on research and development. Business environment variables (46) include port and airport infrastructure quality, police protection of businesses, quality of management schools, ease of access to loans, buyer sophistication, and tariff liberalization.

3. As the time of writing, small parts of the 2003–2004 competitiveness report had become available. The United States slipped to second place among 102 ranked nations, behind Finland (where, in fact, we were in 2001–2002). The slippage appears to be due mainly to a large decline in macroeconomic stability—the WEF looked at all those tax cuts and the shift from a huge budget surplus to a huge deficit and didn't like what it saw. There was also a slippage in the corruption index, no doubt influenced by all of the indicted or to-be-indicted brokerage firms and ex-CEOs. According to the executive summary, our ever-increasing trade deficit, now coupled with a lower dollar, didn't help.

4. *A Nation at Risk.* 1983. Washington, DC: National Commission on Excellence in Education. (p. 7).

5. Biancolli, Amy. 2001. "At Least Our Kids Ask Questions." *Washington Post,* 27 April, A23.

6. Bracey, Gerald W. 2003. "Teachers Around the World." *Phi Delta Kappan* (November): 253–54.

7. van Wolferen, Karel. 1989. *The Enigma of Japanese Power.* New York: Pan McMillan.

8. French, Howard. 2001. "Hypothesis: Science Gap; Cause: Japan's Ways." *New York Times*, 7 August, A6.

9. Brood, William J. 2004. "U.S. Losing Its Dominance in the Sciences." *New York Times*, 3 May, A1.

10. World Economic Forum (WEF). 2003. *Global Competitiveness Report, 2002–2003*. Geneva: WEF.

Poverty
Grinding Down Achievement

What do I say when people say, "Poverty is no excuse. High-poverty schools can achieve high academic performance"?

You say, "You're right. Poverty is not an excuse. Poverty is a condition, like gravity. Gravity affects everything we do. So does poverty."

If the gravity metaphor doesn't work for you, try this: an ecological system. David K. Shipler, author of the recent *Working Poor: Invisible in America,* had this to say about poverty:

> Some educators and other specialists speak of a "culture of poverty" as if it were a collection of mores, values and rituals. But poverty is not a culture. It's more like an ecological system of relationships among individuals, families and the environment of schools, neighborhoods, jobs and government services. Professionals who aid the poor witness the toxic interactions every day. Doctors see patients affected by dangerous housing, erratic work schedules, transportation difficulties and poor child-rearing skills. Teachers see pupils undermined by violence at home and malnutrition.[1]

The world puts poor children at risk from the start. Their mothers are less likely to receive adequate prenatal care, especially in the first trimester of pregnancy, and this can affect their cognitive performance later in life. Poor kids are more likely to be

> *The world puts poor children at risk from the start.*

physically and/or emotionally abused. They are three times more likely to have stunted growth. They are twice as likely to have physical or mental disabilities. Poor children are more likely to have serious illnesses. They are more likely to drown, suffocate, or die in a fire. The death rate for poor children is three times that for other kids.[2] Name your childhood risk, it's much more likely to punish poor kids.

If the home and community environments alone didn't put poor kids at risk, they often end up in schools that are badly underresourced. Consider these conditions:

- classes in which teachers encourage children to bring boom boxes and headphones from home to drown out the noise from nearby machines
- schools with limited language, science, and mathematics offerings and no laboratories for any of the three subjects
- schools with obsolete textbooks or too few textbooks to assign homework
- schools with no guidance or support staff and pupil–teacher ratios of 43 to 1
- schools where termites have eaten through books, shelves, and school records
- schools whose septic tanks have been condemned for large dark spots on the playgrounds but that allow the kids to play there anyway
- schools where young children pick up beer bottles, condoms, and bullets on school grounds—officials take children out of reading instruction to perform this "beautification work"
- schools where rats scurry about among the bread racks in cafeterias and run through the dining rooms
- schools with chemistry labs that have no chemicals, where literature classes have no books, where computer classes have no computers—where, as one student put it, "We sit there and talk about what we would be doing if we had computers"
- schools where some classes have no teachers and a parade of substitutes show movies
- schools where students are forced to stand in class or sit on windowsills until enough kids leave so that all students have chairs

The first six of these examples come from a 1990 legal brief filed in an equity suit in Alabama (there are dozens of examples in the brief). But before you shake your head over yet more travesties from the intractably backward Deep South, consider that the second five examples come from a class action suit filed in the Golden State of California in 2001. Claire Cooper of the *Sacramento Bee* reported that the depositions filed on behalf of poor districts contained many such "snapshots of filth, chaos and desperation."[3]

In recent years, the Right has used the statement "Poverty is no excuse" as code to mean "Getting poverty-stricken children to achieve at high levels is easy, so there is no excuse for it not to happen everywhere and soon. That it hasn't happened, that students in impacted neighborhoods score low on tests, means that public schools in poor neighborhoods have failed and, therefore, we need vouchers so children can attend better, that is, private, schools."

Two well-known studies allegedly have found schools with high poverty and/or minority enrollment rates that also have high test scores. The Education Trust conducted one of these studies, the Heritage Foundation the other. I'll take each in turn, then present some poverty-related data from PIRLS (Progress in International Reading Literacy Study) released in April 2003 by the International Association for the Evaluation of Educational Achievement, the same organization that conducted TIMSS. Somehow, the acronym for this Hague-based institution is always given as IEA, and I follow that convention here.

In setting out to dispel the myth that poverty schools cannot be, in its term, *high-flying schools* (sometimes also referred to by the Trust as *great schools*), the Education Trust looked at the test results in all states. The Trust developed criteria for high performance and, using them, claimed to have found 4,577 high flyers. Of these, 3,592 were high-poverty schools and 2,305 were high-minority schools.[4]

Only 1,320 of the high-scoring schools were both high poverty and high minority. Thus, even by its own criteria, the Trust did not find many high-flying schools that were high both in poverty levels and minority enrollment: about 1.5 percent of all schools.

When one looks at the Trust's criteria for high-flying schools, though, one must conclude that they cruise at a considerably

lower altitude than the Trust claimed. To be designated as high
flying, schools had to have 50 percent or more minority enrollment or 50 percent or more students in poverty (or both) and had
to score in the upper third of the state on the statewide test, whatever test that might be. The Trust defined high poverty as the percent eligible for free and reduced-price meals. Because families
earning up to 185 percent of poverty are eligible, this is a fairly
lenient criterion for poverty. The 2004 federal definition of
poverty is $18,850 for a family of four, meaning that the same
family of four today can earn up to $34,873 and still be eligible
for low-cost meals.[5] But it is the proxy measure for poverty that is
most readily available and most often used. It does underestimate
the percent of kids in poverty at the high school level, where
many students do not want to admit to being poor, but virtually
none of the Trust's high flyers were high schools.

To be high flying, a school had to land in the upper third of
the state only in

  one year,
  one grade, and
  one subject.

That is, if, in a given school, the fourth grade scored in the upper
third on the state reading (or math or language) test for any one
year, the school received the designation high flying. These are
hardly stringent criteria. Stephen Krashen, professor emeritus at
the University of Southern California, observed that even these
low criteria were misleading. For some of the schools he was
familiar with, the schools owed their accolades to the middle-
class students who attended them. The poor children in the
schools did not do well at all.[6] (As an aside, the one good feature
of the No Child Left Behind law is that it forces schools to disag-
gregate test data by ethnicity and socioeconomic status.)

The Education Trust maintains an interactive database of the
numbers it used and anyone can manipulate the variables and
determine results (*www.edtrust.org*). People can set their own criteria and see what happens from any state they choose to analyze.
Because the Education Trust had already performed a separate
analysis for California,[7] and because California has used the same
test for several years (thus scores would not be depressed from

the imposition of an unfamiliar test nor overstated from using the same test for too many years), and because California is a big state (thus, scores would be less susceptible to much fluctuation from year to year), I analyzed California data.

The Trust had identified 355 California high flyers with high poverty, 300 with high minority enrollments, and 143 with both. At the time of the study, California operated 8,761 schools. Thus the Education Trust's criteria designated only 1.6 percent of California schools as high flyers, using both poverty and minority enrollment.

The Education Trust's database permits one to analyze data for up to five years. I decided to define "high flying" to mean schools that scored in the upper quartile (upper 25 percent) of the state, in reading, and at the fourth grade. The database does not permit a simultaneous search using more than one grade or more than one subject. I varied the poverty level and determined the number of high-flying schools as poverty grew and the number of such schools that were able to sustain that status for additional years. The results are shown below.

School Poverty Rate	# Schools	High Flyers 2003–2004	2 Years	3 Years	4 Years	5 Years
All	4,914	1,260	949	823	740	664
10%	4,393	677	485	398	342	291
25%	3,716	249	139	109	79	58
50%	2,693	38	14	10	6	4
75 %	1,479	6	1	1	0	0
90 %	639	1	0	0	0	0

Thus we can readily see that only a tiny fraction of schools with any significant amount of poverty can attain high-flying status and few of those can sustain that level over time. For example, of the 3,716 schools that had 25 percent or more of their students living in poverty, only 249 or 0.6 percent attained high-flying status and only 58 of those were able to sustain that status for another four years. After the poverty level reaches 75 percent, there are virtually no high-flying schools and only one could sustain the status for another two years. One can only imagine how few schools the search would have identified if the database permitted it to use two subjects or two grades simultaneously.

The Education Trust database, then, far from "dispelling the myth" actually provides compelling evidence that the so-called myth is firmly grounded in reality.

The Heritage Foundation's *No Excuses* report presents a much less formal study.[8] It extracts some general traits of its twenty-one high-performing schools, then offers vignettes of each. The report does not specify how the traits were extracted from the vignettes and some of the vignettes contradict some of the traits. For instance, one extracted trait holds that "master teachers bring out the best in a faculty." Yet only one vignette even mentions master teachers and not in connection with "bringing out the best." Another school not only does not make use of master teachers, but deliberately hires uncertified teachers. In yet another, teachers seem little more than acolytes of the principal.

All of the schools have test scores above the sixty-fifth percentile and 75 percent or more of their students are eligible for free or reduced-price meals. If one assumes that the proportion of low-income schools is roughly the same as the proportion of children living in poverty—a highly conservative assumption—then there are some 19,000 low-income schools. (The nation contains about 95,000 schools and currently about 20 percent of all children live in poverty.) The study found twenty-one high-performing low-income schools.

Some of the test scores reported are simply too high to be real—averages at the ninety-eighth and ninety-ninth percentiles. The only school I know that scores as high as some of those reported in *No Excuses* is the Thomas Jefferson High School for Science and Technology in Fairfax County, Virginia. Fairfax is a large (160,000-student), high-scoring district. It selects about four hundred of the highest scorers in the district each year for Thomas Jefferson's freshman class. These four hundred elite students, as a group, actually do score at the ninety-eighth and ninety-ninth percentiles.

If we ignore the artificial test scores for the moment, there are traits of the schools that probably do contribute to high performance but which are not extracted as traits by the report:

1. *Effort.* The principals work hard and expect teachers to do the same. Indeed, for some of the schools, one wonders what kind of life apart from the school the teachers or the principal

can have. One school gives kids cell phones and their teachers' home numbers. While this no doubt helps achievement, one can wonder how many people would be willing to put up with constant intrusion into their personal lives. One principal even admits that to replicate his school on a large scale would require a "whole species of educators that do not currently exist."

It is wonderful that some people have dedicated themselves so completely to the education of disadvantaged students, but one must wonder how large the pool of such dedicatees is.

2.   *Money.* The report plays coy about money, but clearly some schools receive substantial supplemental funds from outside sources such as businesses and foundations. A press release for one company stated, "We [Johnson Controls] are pleased to join Chrysler, Ford, General Motors and many other corporate sponsors in this worthwhile effort." At another school, salaries began at $31,000 for teachers with a bachelor's degree and $35,000 for those with a master's in a locale where most public schools in the region started at $22,000.

If money is not important, as conservative school critics are wont to say, one wonders why so many of the *No Excuses* schools need income over and above that provided by their districts.

3.   *Time.* Many of the schools operate on an eleven-month year and a six-day week, with after-school programs as well.

4.   *Size.* Most of the schools are small. There is considerable evidence now that all else being equal, small schools produce higher achievement than large ones.[9]

5.   *Selectivity.* The *No Excuses* schools select students in a variety of ways. Some have high tuition. Some are private schools and select whomever they please. Some do not offer transportation, making them available only to parents with access to transportation, the money to pay for it, and the flexibility of time to use it.

These factors likely affect the academic outcomes. In addition, the report omits some factors that also might be important. Parts of the report do not clearly specify poverty-level data, funding, staff qualifications, test scores, or the fate of the students once they leave the school. This last is important because the *No*

Excuses schools, like those in the Education Trust study, are almost exclusively elementary schools. Test scores can be manipulated in elementary schools much more easily than in middle and high schools. It is important to know if the higher test scores hold up in the students' later academic careers, but *No Excuses* provides no longitudinal data. In the absence of such, one should be skeptical.

A more extensive analysis of *No Excuses* can be found in *On the Death of Childhood and the Destruction of Public Schools.*[10]

Two recent international studies also provided information that bears on poverty and performance. These are PIRLS, from 2003 and PISA, from 2001 (see *www.nces.ed.gov/surveys/pirls* and *www.nces.ed.gov/surveys/pisa*).

The U.S. Department of Education analyzed PIRLS data by percent of students in poverty, again defined by eligibility for free or reduced-price meals. The three columns show, in order: the percent of students in poverty in schools, the average score of those students, and the percent of all U.S. students who fall into each category:

Percent of Students in Poverty	Score	Percent of All U.S. Students in Category
<10	589	13
10–25	567	17
25–50	551	28
50–75	518	22
75+	485	20
Top Nation, Sweden	561	
United States	543	
International Average	500	

Thus, the top two categories of schools scored higher than the highest of the thirty-five nations participating in the study. If schools with 25 percent to 50 percent of their students in poverty constituted a nation, it would rank fourth among those thirty-five nations. Indeed, only students in schools with 75 percent poverty scored below the international average of 500.

People have tried to define *world-class* in general terms, without a great deal of success, but it seems to me that when 30 percent of students (the first two categories) finish first in the world among thirty-five mostly industrialized countries and another 28 percent rank fourth, that's a pretty good operational definition.

The results from 2001's PISA are equally dramatic although cast in a different metric. Students in all countries were assigned scores from 16 to 90 depending on parents' socioeconomic status (SES). It is not possible from the PISA data to calculate the actual scores for different SES levels, but we can calculate the relative score. If we assume an American student with the lowest SES number scored at the international average of 500, then an American student with the highest SES would score 660, or at the ninety-fifth percentile. Conversely, if we assume that an American student with the highest SES number scored at the international average, then a student with the lowest SES would score 340, or at the fifth percentile. For those familiar with the statistical properties of the normal curve, the difference between the highest and lowest SES numbers converts to a score differential of 1.6 standard deviations. The differences are huge.

Money matters.

Notes

1. Shipler, David K. 2004. "Total Poverty Awareness." *New York Times,* 27 February, A15.

2. *Helping Families Work.* 1994. Columbus, OH: Ohio Children's Defense Foundation.

3. Cooper, Claire. 2001. "Lawsuit Offers Litany of School Woes." *Sacramento Bee,* 21 September.

4. Education Trust. 2001 and 2003. *Dispelling the Myth.* www.edtrust.org.

5. National Center for Children in Poverty frequently asked questions: *www.nccp.org/faq.html.*

6. Krashen, Stephen. 2002. "Don't Trust the Education Trust." *Substance* (February): 3.

7. Ali, Russlyn, and Craig D. Jerald. 2001. *Dispelling the Myth in California.* Washington, DC: Education Trust.

8. Carter, Samuel Casey. 2001. *No Excuses: Lessons from Twenty-One High-Performing, High Poverty Schools.* Washington, DC: Heritage Foundation.

9. Wasley, Patricia, Linda C. Farrell, Esther Mosak, Sherry P. King, Nicole E. Holland, Matt Gladden, and Michelle Fine. 2000. *Small Schools, Great Strides—A Study of New Small Schools in Chicago*. New York: Banks Street College of Education.

10. Bracey, Gerald W. 2003. *On the Death of Childhood and the Destruction of Public Schools: The Folly of Today's Education Policies and Practices*. Portsmouth, NH: Heinemann.

"Plummeting" SAT Scores

What do I say when someone says, "SAT scores have plummeted"?

You can say, "No, they haven't." People who say the scores have plummeted are invariably critics of the schools who use emotion-laden words like plummet, plunge, *and* nose-dive *to persuade rather than to convey facts.*

I f you take into account the demographic changes in who has been taking the SAT, SAT scores have changed little since 1951.[1] In fact, it would not be too flippant to say "Hooray!" The decline in SAT scores reflected, more than anything else, changes in who was coming to college. The standards for the SAT were set in 1941 on a group made up mostly of affluent white males from prep schools in the Northeast. In the 1960s, the civil rights and women's movements caused colleges to open their doors to a wider range of students. Scores fell. Hooray. It was a victory for civil rights. Harold Howe, a former commissioner of education in the federal government, penned an article titled "Let's Have Another SAT Decline," indicating that the triumph was not complete.[2]

> *If you take into account the demographic changes in who has been taking the SAT, SAT scores have changed little since 1951.*

In *The Big Test: The Secret History of the American Meritocracy,* Nicholas Lemann argued that the SAT had become *the* all-powerful determinant of people's status in the culture.[3] Lemann was wrong, but he certainly captured what people *think* about the SAT's power. About the time his book appeared, a cartoon in *USA Today* showed a mother sitting on the side of her child's bed, reading to her. The mother says, "And the little pig with the higher SAT scores lived happily ever after, but the other pigs were eaten by the wolf."[4]

This perception of the SAT as the only thing that counts stands in sharp contrast to how the SAT's developers viewed it (and how college admissions officers actually view it today).

This perception of the SAT as the only thing that counts stands in sharp contrast to how the SAT's developers viewed it (and how college admissions officers actually view it today). The SAT creators had much more modest goals for it. The SAT's principal author, Carl Campbell Brigham, had this to say about it in 1926, its maiden year:

> The present state of all efforts of men to measure or in any way estimate the worth of other men, or to evaluate the results of their nurture, or to reckon their potential possibilities does not warrant any certainty of prediction . . . This additional test now made available through the instrumentality of the College Entrance Examination Board may help to resolve a few perplexing problems, but it should be regarded merely as a supplementary record. To place too great emphasis on test scores is as dangerous as the failure to properly evaluate any score or rank in conjunction with other measures and estimates which it supplements.[5]

Mere supplement. Would that people held that view today. In fact, some of us have argued that the SAT is *so* supplementary it isn't even worth the time and cost. It tells the colleges nothing they don't know from the rest of the high school record, doesn't help students choose a college, and operates to the detriment of minority and poor students.[6, 7] Robert Schaefer of FairTest once told me that when he addresses college admissions officers, he asks for a show of hands of how many of them would still require the SAT if the colleges rather than the students had to pay for it. Schaefer said he has yet to see a hand in the air. The colleges collect the data because it is free and because, if the scores are high enough, they can be used to both liberate money from alumni and recruit students to attend.

The College Board, known then as the College Entrance Examination Board, introduced the SAT to replace the subject matter essay exams the Board had given since its founding in

1900. The predictive power of tests developed during World War I had impressed the Board. Frederick J. Kelly of the University of Kansas invented the multiple-choice test item in 1915, providing for the first time a format that made mass standardized testing possible and relatively quick and cheap to produce. Psychologists put that format to use during World War I to select people for various duty stations. The original SAT contained essay as well as multiple-choice questions, but the essays were dropped in 1941 (the entry of the U.S. into World War II interfered with the administration of the essay portion).

The Board scaled the raw scores (percent correct) onto a six-hundred-point scale that ranged from 200 to 800 points. It assigned the average raw score a scaled score of 500 points. The standard deviation, a measure of how scores vary around the average, was set to 100. These are straightforward statistical procedures, not something done with smoke and mirrors although one can wonder about the wisdom of spreading tests with ninety questions (verbal) and sixty questions (mathematics) onto such a large scale.[8] In the math test, for example, each question would be worth ten points.[9] If one person got two questions more correct than another, that would likely mean nothing, but converted to a scaled score, the difference would be 20 points, and a number that size *looks* significant.

Who were those standard setters in 1941? They were 10,654 students mostly living in New England and New York. Ninety-eight percent of them were white, 61 percent were male, and 41 percent had attended private college-preparatory high schools. They were, in a phrase, an elite. It was the average raw score of these elite that received a scaled score of 500.

By 1951, the average verbal score had fallen to 476, where it remained until the Great SAT Decline that began in 1963. The mathematics score (at the time, called quantitative) remained steady near 500.

No one has ever addressed this earlier slide of the SAT verbal, probably because no one can explain it. No major curriculum changes affected the schools except for Life Adjustment Education, which educators specifically created for students who would not attend college. Television had not permeated the culture. Families were intact. The country was about to enter the "togetherness" years of the Eisenhower administration. The year

1952 would see the first installment of a television series that would define and represent this period, *Ozzie and Harriet.* Only jazz musicians and a few marginalized groups were using drugs recreationally. The decline might have come as a consequence of something else widely perceived as a civil rights triumph, the GI Bill of Rights, which permitted any World War II veteran to attend college. Many who used the bill could not otherwise have afforded to attend an institution of higher education.

In 1963, one year before the landmark Civil Rights Act of 1964, the SAT began what would be a twenty-year decline in the average score. The SAT verbal fell from 476 to 423, the math from 500 to 468. The general public at first did not notice the fall: the SAT was of interest to the students in the Northeast and Atlantic Seaboard South planning to attend institutions of higher educa-tion, to their counselors, and to college admissions officers. The College Board noticed, though, and in 1976 appointed a panel headed by former Secretary of Labor Willard Wirtz and former Commissioner of Education Harold Howe to study the matter.

The panel's report, *On Further Examination,* attributed most of the decline from 1963 to 1970 to changes in who was showing up to take the test: more women, more minorities, more students from families with limited economic means, more students with mediocre high school grades, and more students lacking a strong high school course-taking record. The panel claimed that these changes had stabilized by 1972, so other factors had to be found to account for the further fall (staff to the panel contended that the demographic changes had *not* stabilized).[10]

And did the panel find factors! One background paper for the panel simply listed the hypotheses that various theorists and groups had brought forward to explain the decline. They had brought forth seventy-nine such hypotheses, many of them plau-sible. They run the gamut of societal, familial, curricular, instruc-tional, and motivational possibilities. If each hypothesis explained only one point of the decline, virtually all of it would be accounted for. The panel also cast some of the blame on a "decade of distraction," which included not only ubiquitous tele-vision but events such as the assassinations of John F. Kennedy, Robert Kennedy, Martin Luther King Jr., and Malcolm X; the civil rights movement; the free speech movement; the Watts riots in Los Angeles and the urban unrest that followed all across the nation; the riots at the 1968 Democratic national convention; the Vietnam War; Watergate; and the general "making of a counterculture" that rejected many traditional values, including achievement in school (many other indicators of achievement fell during this same period).

Since the panel's report, further relevant demographic changes have occurred. Large numbers of immigrants have entered the United States from Southeast Asia, Mexico, Central and South America, and eastern Europe. During this period, the SAT scores have stabilized for the verbal test and have increased somewhat for the math (both scores rose in 2003). When SATs are examined by ethnicity, however, all groups show gains on both the verbal and the mathematics tests (see pages 152 to 159 for an explanation of this paradoxical result).

The panel's report transformed the SAT from a mere supplement into front-page news. Every microscopic change landed on page 1 and in prime time—at least when the scores went down. In recent years, when scores have been stable or increased, papers such as the *New York Times* have stuffed the results deep in the front section, while the *Washington Post* put the story in its Metro section, something of only local interest. One year the *Washington Post* waited until the eighth paragraph of the article to reveal the national results.

The Notorious 1995 SAT "Recentering"

The publishers of norm-referenced achievement tests such as the SAT-9 (SAT here stands for Stanford Achievement Tests), the Terra Nova, and the Iowa Tests of Basic Skills periodically "renorm" their tests. Curricula change, teachers and students become familiar with the questions and these factors drive the norms into obsolescence. The norm in most norm-referenced tests is a floating standard—the score of the average student in the renorming sample, whatever that score might be.[11] By contrast, standards on the SAT were fixed in 1941.

The elite that set these standards never really represented who went to college, not even in New England, where most of the standard setters resided. As years went by and a larger and larger proportion of high school graduates aspired to attend institutions of higher education, the 500 on the SAT less and less meaning-fully reflected the score of the average college-bound high school senior.

People misinterpreted the scores. Students who received, say, a 450 on their SAT verbal considered themselves below average. Their perception was accurate but only in reference to the 1941 standard setters, not in reference to their contemporaries. In 1995, the College Board renormed the SAT, but, because the College Board likes to consider itself unique, it called its renorm-ing *recentering*. The Board once again scaled the average raw score to 500. This 500, though, represented the average score of more than one million seniors who took the SAT that year. The differ-ence between the two scales was large for the verbal test and small for mathematics. In fact, there is a range from 660 to 710 on the mathematics, where test takers actually score 10 points *lower* on the new scale.

School critics howled. They accused the College Board of hid-ing ignorance. Former Assistant Secretary of Education Chester Finn called it "the greatest dose of educational Prozac ever admin-istered." To me, it seemed the most reasonable thing for the College Board to do to render SAT scores in their proper perspec-tive. If a student got a 500 on the SAT in 2003, he or she really was average or close to it among 1,406,324 seniors who took the test that year, but, of course, not among the 10,654 select students who set the standard in 1941.[12]

Notes

1. Bracey, Gerald W. 1990. "SAT Scores: Miserable or Miraculous?" *Education Week* (21 November). However, ethnic changes in the SAT test-taking pool have obscured gains in the last twenty years. See Chapter 11.

2. Howe, Harold II. 1985. "Let's Have Another SAT Decline." *Phi Delta Kappan* (May): 599–602.

3. Lemann, Nicholas. 1999. *The Big Test: The Secret History of the American Meritocracy.* New York: Farrar, Strauss & Giroux.

4. That selective colleges use other factors than the SAT can be seen

by looking at their admissions records. Brown University, for instance, could fill two freshman classes just with students scoring between 750 and 800 on the SAT verbal. It accepts fewer than a third of these students and accepts some students with 400s on the SAT.

5. Angoff, William H. 1971. *The College Entrance Examination Board Testing Programs: A Technical Report.* New York: The College Entrance Examination Board.

6. Crouse, James, and Dale Trusheim. 1988. *The Case Against the SAT.* Chicago: University of Chicago Press.

7. Bracey, Gerald W. 1989. "The $150 Million Redundancy." *Phi Delta Kappan* (May): 698–702.

8. Scaled scores abound, although people are not aware of their presence. IQ scores are scaled scores, as are scores from the National Assessment of Educational Progress and from all of the various international comparisons of test scores. In fact, the international comparisons use the same scale as the SAT. Readers interested in learning how scaled scores are constructed or more about the SAT can find both discussed in my book *Put to the Test: An Educator's and Consumer's Guide to Standardized Tests* (Phi Delta Kappa International, 2002).

9. This is not precisely accurate because some of the questions are worth a little more than some others.

10. Beaton, Albert. 1998. Personal communication. At the time of the panel's investigation, Beaton was a statistician at Educational Testing Service and served as a staff member to the panel.

11. The norms used to be truly floating standards as testing companies, save for the publishers of the Iowa Tests of Basic Skills, made no links between new and older editions of the tests. Equating methods and the need for longitudinal data have led all publishers to provide such links now.

12. With an ever-increasing percentage of high school seniors taking the SAT and with a growing number of seniors as the baby boomlet moves through school, it is not possible to say precisely how a 500 score stacks up.

The Shrinking SAT Elite

What do I say when people say, "The proportion of students who score high on the SAT is getting smaller and smaller"?

You can say, "No it isn't. The proportion of high scorers on the SAT verbal has increased somewhat in recent years, and the proportion of high scorers on the SAT math has hit a new record high almost every single year since 1981. And that growth is not due to high-scoring Asian kids."

Trend data on highscorers first appeared in 1976 as a background paper for *On Further Examination*. The data started with the school year 1966–1967.[1] Rex Jackson, an ETS researcher, grouped the data in one-hundred-point intervals so analyses of the results cannot be too refined or precise. In 1966, the third year of the SAT's twenty-year fall, 2.3 percent of the students scored above 700 on the SAT verbal and in 2003, 1.2 percent attained such scores. We also know, from the statistical properties of the normal curve, that 2.3 percent of the standard setters in 1941 scored above 700 (a score of 700 is two standard deviations above the mean and only 2.3 percent of the scores are at this level or above). Thus the proportion of superhigh scorers has been roughly halved. However, 1966 appears to have been the last high year and the fall occurred very fast. By 1968, the proportion of students scoring 700 or better was 1.8 percent, and by 1972, it was 1.1 percent. The proportion appears to have stabilized at 1.1 or 1.2 percent from 1972 to the present, using the old scale.

As noted, the recentering left the math test largely unaffected. In 1966, 3.9 percent of students scored above 700 on the math test, and by 1975, that proportion had fallen to 3.1 percent. The proportion started rising then and by 1995, it was at 5.6 percent, an all-time high. If the recentering did anything to the math, it made it slightly harder, and in 1996, 5.4 percent of students scored 700 or better. By 2002, this proportion had climbed to 6.3 percent, another all-time high.

What accounts for the difference between the verbal trend and the math trend? No direct answers are obvious, but several factors suggest themselves. One is television. David Berliner of Arizona State University contends that starting in the early 1960s, our major form of recreation changed and we spent more and more time in front of the tube and less time reading.[2] This is plausible. In fact, I recall one commentator in the 1960s observed that if situation comedies, which had become all the rage, actually depicted typical American families, they would all show people sitting in the dark watching television.

It is also true that over at least the last twenty to twenty-five years, an increasing number of students who do not speak English as their native language have taken the SAT. Keep in mind that the SAT is a subtle test and keep in mind as well that for the SAT to be "successful," it must trick large numbers of even native English speakers into choosing the wrong answer. Nonnative speakers who can cope with spoken English and are competent even in the English needed for classroom assignments will likely have more difficulty with the SAT.

> *Keep in mind that the SAT is a subtle test and keep in mind as well that for the SAT to be "successful," it must trick large numbers of even native English speakers into choosing the wrong answer.*

Other analyses of the SAT "elite" have used a slightly less aristocratic definition, usually including students scoring 650 or better. A score of 700 on the SAT corresponds to the ninety-eighth percentile, while 650 corresponds to the ninety-second.

One analysis at the 650 level produced a sequence of events that is illustrative of the critics' syndrome I refer to as neurotic need to believe the worst and of a parallel case of exceptionalism—whenever the data look good, school critics invoke some exceptional reason to explain that outcome.

The analysis first appeared in Feburary 1993 in *Education Week*. In that month, *Education Week* began a multipart series, "From Risk to Renewal."[3] *Ed Week* timed the series to culminate at the tenth anniversary of *A Nation at Risk*, which occurred in

April 1993. The series asked what the reforms had accomplished in the ten years since that document had appeared. In the opening joint editorial essay, the editors answered, "Not much":

> The proportion of American youngsters performing at high levels remains infinitesimally small. In the past 10 years, for instance, the number and proportion of those scoring at or above 650 on the verbal or math section of the Scholastic Aptitude Test has actually declined.

In the margin near the text, the editors presented a table of numbers that appeared to confirm their contention. The table looked like this:

Number (and Proportion) of Students Scoring Above 650 on the SAT Verbal and Mathematics, According to *Education Week*

	1982	1992
Verbal	29,921 (3)	22,754 (2)
Math	70,352 (7)	58,662 (6)

These numbers certainly do present the case that both the numbers and the proportions, in parentheses, have declined. But something about these numbers seemed strange to me. It might have been a dim memory that after *A Nation at Risk* appeared in 1983, more students began to take more mathematics and science courses in high school. More courses but fewer high scorers? Not reasonable.

I consulted my collection of *Profiles of College Bound Seniors,* a booklet (now online) that the College Board distributes each year as it releases the latest SAT results. I found the numbers for 1982 accurate. The numbers for 1992 were accurate as far as they went, but they didn't go far enough.

The profiles present the SAT results in a table that groups students by intervals. One sees at the bottom of the table all of the students who scored 200 to 240, then those who scored 250 to 290, 300 to 340, and so forth on up to 750 to 800 (800 being the highest possible score). *Education Week*'s 1992 numbers contain only the number and proportion of students scoring between 650 and 690, totally omitting everyone who scored between 700 and 800. When these numbers are added, a radically different picture emerges:

Number (and Proportion) of Students Actually Scoring Above 650 on the SAT Verbal and Mathematics

	1982	1992
Verbal	29,921 (3)	32,903 (3)
Math	70,352 (7)	104,401 (10)

I wrote *Education Week* requesting a front-page correction. The editors printed no correction at all but did run my letter in the Letters section. To my letter, they appended an editorial note stating that it was still a tiny proportion. I thus had to write a second letter advising the editors that the standards for the SAT were set on the elite group of students described on page 55 and that we know from statistical properties of the normal curve that only 6.68 percent of this nobility scored above 650. But now, in 1992, we had a polyglot group of more than one million test takers that included 29 percent minority students, 52 percent females, and 83 percent public school students (recall that 41 percent of the standard setters attended private, college-prep high schools).

The proportion of SAT takers scoring above 650 was one of many statistics I included in a *Washington Post* op-ed essay.[4] There it was seen by conservative school critic Denis Doyle. When the Heritage Foundation assigned Doyle the education chapter of *Issues '96: The Candidates' Briefing Book,* a tome the Heritage Foundation publishes each presidential election year, he used the occasion to take issue with my analysis in a section about it called "Chicken Little in Reverse":

> American education continues to be in crisis. Government spending has skyrocketed even as school performance and student achievement have remained static, leaving young Americans ill equipped to function in today's increasingly competitive world. The liberal solution, as always, is more money, more bureaucracy, more federal intrusion. [*Author's note:* Doyle appears to relish the federal intrusion from George W. Bush's No Child Left Behind initiative.]
>
> On December 22, 1995, the *Washington Post* ran an op-ed by Gerald A. [sic] Bracey, a professional critic of the critics, arguing that things have never been better, that "scores on many commercial achievement tests" and the "proportion of students scoring above 650 on the SAT mathematics test (on the old scale) are at an all time high."

He does not tell the reader who is pushing the SAT math scores higher, mostly Asian and Asian-American students.

Candidates for public office should not be fooled by fatuous assertions that test scores are climbing.[5]

Perhaps because Doyle considered them "fatuous assertions," he did not bother to provide any evidence to support his claim that increasing numbers of Asian American students produced the increase in high scorers. Here resides the exceptionalism that I mentioned earlier. Doyle claims that if things are improving, it can't be because the *system* is actually getting better. The improvement must derive from some exceptional condition, in this case the presence of increasing numbers of Asian test takers.

To make an assertion but not provide any data is, at best, to formulate a hypothesis. Doyle had not tested his hypothesis. I decided to test it for him. I obtained the SAT scores by ethnicity from the College Board. Overall, the results look like this:

High Scorers (Above 650)
SAT Mathematics

	1981	1995
Number	70,307	132,898
Percent	7.1	12.4
Percent Growth	74.6	

Doyle's hypothesis contends that Asian American students produced the gain. Therefore, if I removed the Asian students from the sample, then the 75 percent overall gain should disappear or become quite small. It does not, as seen in the following table.

High Scorers (Above 650)
SAT Mathematics
Without Asian Students[6]

	1981	1995
Number	65,672	118,879
Percent	6.8	10.7
Percent Growth	57.3	

The gain does shrink because Asian American students do score higher than any other ethnic group (in 2003, almost precisely one-third scored above 650). But there was a 57 percent gain for black, white, Hispanic, and Native American students over the period from 1981 to 1995. Score one for fatuous assertions.

For the record, the following tables bring the data up to date:

High Scorers (Above 650)
SAT Mathematics

	1981		2003
Number	70,307		207,230
Percent	7.1		14.7
Percent Growth		107	

High Scorers (Above 650)
SAT Mathematics
Without Asian Students

	1981		2003
Number	65,672		142,709
Percent	6.8		11.4
Percent Growth		67	

As for the verbal score, the proportion of high scorers (650 and above) bottomed out in 1983 and has since recovered somewhat, hovering now around 4 percent, using the original scale. It would have to climb back to 6.68 percent to match the 1941 standard setters.

In sum, over the last twenty years, the proportion of students scoring high on the SAT mathematics has been growing virtually every year and setting a new record each time it grows. The proportion of high scorers on the SAT verbal has grown somewhat in that twenty-year period. It seems unlikely that the abbreviated, codelike English common in e-mails, chat rooms, and blogs will elevate the proportion—or the discourse.

Notes

1. Jackson, Rex. 1976. "An Examination of Declining Numbers of High-Scoring SAT Candidates." Paper prepared for the Advisory Panel

of the Scholastic Aptitude Test Decline. Jackson was an ETS researcher serving as staff to the panel.

2. Berliner argues that the SAT has probably *increased* the working vocabulary of Americans. Who before this century knew such recently common words as *recuse* and *anthrax*. But the SAT is a literary English test in part and, despite the efforts of Oprah and the various cities adopting books to read, television has likely had a devastating impact on our literary vocabularies.

3. *Education Week* editorial staff. 1993. "From Risk to Renewal." *Education Week* (10 February).

4. Bracey, Gerald W. 1995. "American Students: Better than Ever." *Washington Post,* 22 December, A19.

5. Doyle, Dennis P. 1996. "Education." In *Issues '96: The Candidates' Briefing Book,* 261–95. Washington, DC: Heritage Foundation.

6. The analyses by ethnicity use slightly different numbers than the analyses for the entire group because some takers do not provide their ethnic group. Indeed, one 2004 article reports that the number of students refusing to provide ethnic data is now so large that ethnic comparisons might no longer be valid. See Whittington, Dale. 2004. "The Achievement Gap: Should We Rely on SAT Scores to Tell Us Anything About It?" *Education Policy Analysis Archives* 12 (12): *http://epaa.asu .edu/epaa/v12n12.*

6 No Child Left Behind
The Perfect Law—as in The Perfect Storm

What do I say when people say, "President Bush's No Child Left Behind law will force schools to shape up"?

You can say, "The No Child Left Behind law promises to leave even more children behind and to leave public education behind—replaced with a privatized system."

W e're not backing down!" George W. Bush told an audience in Van Buren, Arkansas, on May 11, 2004.[1] He thereby refused to acknowledge criticism of his No Child Left Behind law (officially, the latest version of the Elementary and Secondary Education Act, first passed in 1964). This statement seems likely to become his educational equivalent of "Bring 'em on" and "Mission Accomplished." After all, as Figure 6–1 shows, California projects that by the witching year of 2014, when 100 percent of the nation's students are supposed to be "proficient," 99 percent of the state's schools will be labeled as "failing" under No Child Left Behind (NCLB).

One might reply, "Yes, but that's California, a state so educationally awful it merited a 2004 John Merrow PBS special, *First to Worst: The Rise and Fall of California's Public Schools*." To that the proper retort would be, "Well, then, consider Minnesota." In an article titled "All Minnesota Left Behind?" the *St. Paul Pioneer Press* described a report from the state's Legislative Auditor finding that 80 percent of Minnesota's schools would be failing by 2014.[2] Minnesota is one of the highest scoring states in the country. In TIMSS, only six of forty-one countries outscored it in mathematics and only one in science.

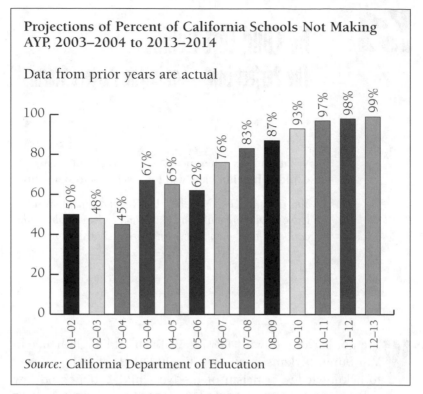

Projections of Percent of California Schools Not Making AYP, 2003–2004 to 2013–2014

Data from prior years are actual

Source: California Department of Education

Figure 6–1. Projections of Percent of California Schools Not Making AYP

Why would anyone, much less a president, dream up a program that flunks everyone? After all, if everyone fails, the program provides no useful information.

At first glance, No Child Left Behind flies in the face of everything the Bush administration stands for, which is mostly deregulating everything and privatizing everything that's in the public sector. An early Bush proposal called for "outsourcing" 850,000 government jobs to the private sector. As this is written, soldiers are still doing most—but not all—of the shooting in Iraq, but Halliburton is doing the rest. One subsidiary alone, KBR, has 20,000 employees in Iraq. Bush rolled back the Clean Air Act using the doublespeak phrase "clear skies," proposed opening the Alaska Wildlife Refuge to drilling, shelved the national ban on the polluting gasoline additive, MBTE, and refused to reauthorize the Superfund tax on polluting industries, thus slowing the pace of polluted site cleanup.

Molly Ivins, the syndicated columnist who has known Bush since high school, and has written two books about him, *Shrub* and *Bushwhacked: Life in George W. Bush's America*, says he is a true Texan. Unlike his faux-Texan father, Bush really is comfortable on the ranch in jeans, cutting brush and exhibiting those three qualities that Ivins claims define Texas males: religiosity, anti-intellectualism, and machismo. Texans like Bush, said Ivins on National Public Radio's *Fresh Air*, think things will be OK if government creates a healthy business climate. In Texas, she contends, "a healthy business" climate means letting corporations do pretty much whatever they want. In fact, Ivins feels Bush's faith in the market is so strong that it is closer to a religious than a political belief.[3]

Yet, from the most antiregulatory administration since before the Great Depression, comes No Child Left Behind (NCLB), eleven hundred pages of straitjacket law, with reams of attendant rules and regulations from the U.S. Department of Education. Why would an antiregulatory administration impose tons of regulations on public schools? Because the goal of NCLB is the destruction of public schools, not their salvation. NCLB sets the schools up to fail and be privatized.

> *The goal of NCLB is the destruction of public schools, not their salvation.*

How will the law lead to privatization? Let me count the ways.

To understand the agenda of NCLB, we must consider the history of the bill. In some drafts, the bill contained voucher provisions. When sent to Congress, though, these provisions had been removed. The White House then instigated voucher amendments, six altogether, introduced by John Boehner (R-Ohio). In this way, removal of the voucher amendments would not be seen as a personal defeat for the president. Congress, mindful that in the 2000 elections voucher referenda had suffered 70–30 defeats in both California and Michigan (despite voucher advocates having outspent opponents 2–1), rejected the amendments.

Congress reasoned, as did a number of others, that there was no widespread market for vouchers. Supporters now said that vouchers would be attractive to some few families trapped in bad urban schools, perhaps 5 percent of all families. "I think maybe the word is part of the problem," said then Senate Majority Leader Trent Lott.[4] "Maybe the word should be *scholarship*." At his Senate hearings confirming him as Secretary of Education, Rod

Paige told the committee, "the word *voucher* has taken on a negative tone."[5]

Negative tone or no, Bush brought vouchers back as a special program for the District of Columbia. The Senate defeated the measure on four occasions, but in January 2004, Bush managed to get the vouchers attached to a $328 billion omnibus spending bill.[6] The Senate was unwilling to scuttle that entire bill simply to keep vouchers out of D.C. During the debate, no one mentioned that an earlier three-year-long voucher program in D.C. had failed to either increase the achievement of students using them above a matched sample of public school students or to get the public schools to improve. Look for broader voucher proposals after the 2004 elections if Bush is successful in his quest for reelection. Bush made his strongest pitch for the program in a White House East Room speech to 250 Catholic educators. Given that Catholic schools will be the principal beneficiary of vouchers, one can see Bush's insistence on getting the program established as a cynical ploy to buy the Catholic vote.

Thus, with the middle classes contentedly rejecting vouchers, to grease the skids for any widespread program, some means had to be found to alienate those middle classes from their schools. This is what NCLB is primed to do through the instrument of Adequate Yearly Progress (AYP). AYP is not a new concept, having been part of the reauthorization of the Elementary and Secondary Education Act in 1998 (which, technically, is what NCLB is, too). But NCLB throws two new curves: (1) schools that fail to make AYP for two or more consecutive years are subject to increasingly harsh sanctions, and (2) all children must score at the "proficient" level or better by 2014. And pigs will fly.

At the moment, each state defines *proficient* and chooses whatever test it wishes, but as we will see soon, there will be pressure to adopt a single definition using only one test, NAEP. Beginning in 2002–2003, NCLB required states to test children in at least one grade in grades 3–5, 6–9, and 10–12. Beginning in 2005–2006, states must test all children every year in grades 3 through 8 in reading and mathematics. In 2007–2008, states must add science in those grades. States must also test at least one high school grade.

Each school must report not only AYP for the school as a whole, but for various ethnic groups, economic categories, special education students, and English Language Learners. At least 95

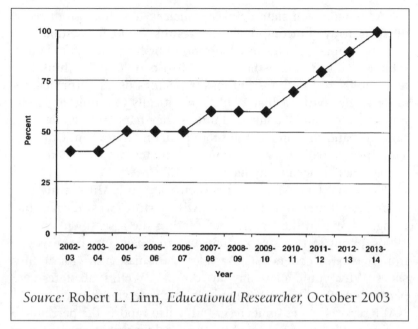

Source: Robert L. Linn, *Educational Researcher,* October 2003

Figure 6–2. Ohio AYP Objectives

percent of each group must show up on test day and bubble in answer sheets. If only 93 percent of, say, special education students take the test, the whole school fails. For most schools, there are some 37 groups to report and if any one of them fails, the whole school fails (the official label is "needs improvement," but no one outside of the Department of Education uses this term).

Each state has developed a plan to get it to the mirage-ical 100 percent proficient by 2014. Many states have opted for plans that require little of them initially, but greatly increased achievement as 2014 approaches, such the plan for Ohio shown in Figure 6–2.

From one perspective, a plan like this bespeaks insanity, from another, it makes perfect sense as a strategy. From the loony side, anyone in education knows that no reform program has ever shown accelerating improvement late in its life. It's like taking out a mortgage with an enormous balloon payment in the final years and hoping the bank is defunct when crunch time actually rolls around.

From the sane perspective, a plan like Ohio's buys the state some time in the early years. The state can then hope that Congress injects a modicum of rationality to the law or that it gets repealed.

As noted, each state defines *proficient*. This has produced a dizzying array of incomprehensible results. In the first estimate of the law's impact, Michigan was found to be home to 1,500 failing schools, while Arkansas had none. Most people didn't think this made any sense in terms of those two states usual performances on tests. But with each state idiosyncratically defining *proficient*, no two states can be compared unless they happen to choose the same test and the same cutoff score to define that term. Unlikely. Thus, people will seek a common measure to compares states one to the other. They already have it: NAEP.

Prior to NCLB, state-level participation in NAEP testing was voluntary. Initially, state-level NAEP testing was illegal, but Congress revised the law in 1988, and in the assessments of the 1990s, about forty states participated and paid for the privilege from the states' coffers. NCLB made NAEP mandatory for all fifty states. Why would a law, any law, do that? Well, if all states take part in NAEP, all states have at least one assessment in common. NAEP reports scores on its tests and it also reports the percentage of students attaining each of its three achievement levels: basic, proficient, and advanced. NAEP already contains the magic word, *proficient*.

NAEP will come to replace the state tests. Indeed, a committee of members of the National Assessment Governing Board was formed in 1991—before the law was enacted—to examine the possibility of using NAEP to "confirm" state test results. The committee's report from March 2002 concludes that such confirmatory use of NAEP is possible.[7] Secretary Paige has already said that he will use NAEP's revelations to "shame" the states into higher performance.[8] Ironically, in a study conducted by the Princeton Review, Texas was found to have the highest discrepancy between NAEP and its state test, which, at the time, was the TAAS (now replaced by the TAKS). Texas claimed 91 percent of its eighth graders were proficient in mathematics, but NAEP awarded that status to only 24 percent of the students.[9]

> *Secretary Paige has already said that he will use NAEP's revelations to "shame" the states into higher performance.*

The NAEP figure of 24 percent of Texas eighth graders proficient hints at a problem: If NAEP becomes the standard, virtually all states will find low percentages of students reaching proficient. Swallowing such discouraging results would be difficult enough if the NAEP judgment were valid. But it is not. The NAEP achievement levels—basic, proficient, and advanced—have been rejected by everyone who has studied them: the General Accounting Office,[10] the National Academy of Education,[11] the National Academy of Sciences,[12] and the Center for Research in Evaluation, Student Standards and Testing (CRESST, co-headquartered at UCLA and the University of Colorado, Boulder),[13] as well as by individual psychometricians such as Lyle V. Jones of the University of North Carolina.

Jones, for instance, pointed out that in TIMSS, American fourth graders were well above the average score among the twenty-six participating nations, but only 18 percent reached proficient and a meager 2 percent attained the vaunted "advanced" status in the NAEP mathematics assessment of the very same year.[14] Jones could have added that only 29 percent reached proficient in the 1996 NAEP science assessment, but American fourth graders were fourth in the world in TIMSS science using percent correct, and third in the word using the TIMSS scaled scores.

It makes no sense. Says Jones, "The average math perform-ance for U.S. fourth graders is significantly above the interna-tional average. When U.S. fourth graders perform well in an inter-national comparison, isn't it unreasonable that only 20 percent are reported by [NAEP] to be 'proficient or better'?" Yes.

Even the NAEP reports damn the NAEP achievement levels with citations from the various reports mentioned above. Consider this from the National Academy of Sciences as cited in the *NAEP 1998 Reading Report Card for the Nation and the States*:

> NAEP's current achievement level setting procedures remain · fundamentally flawed. The judgment tasks are difficult and confusing; raters' judgments of different item types are inter-nally consistent; appropriate validity evidences for the cut scores is lacking; and the process has produced unreasonable results.[15]

Confusing tasks? Internally inconsistent judgments? No validity evidence? These failings would be sufficient to doom any test. Surely none of the for-profit test publishers would *dare* put a test with such properties on the market. So why are we still using the achievement levels? Good question, one so far unanswered, and no one is working to produce anything better.

It gets worse. Recall that all subgroups must make AYP to keep a school from failing. In the 2003 recent NAEP reading assessment, 39 percent of white fourth graders scored proficient or better, while only 10 percent of blacks and 13 percent of Hispanics did so.[16] In math, Asian eighth graders turned in the best performance with 48 percent proficient while only 5 percent of black eighth graders reached the proficient level.[17] And all groups will be 100 percent proficient by 2014? Dream on.

CRESST's co-directors Robert Linn and Eva Baker along with Damian Betebenner observed that getting all students to NAEP's *basic* level would constitute an enormous challenge.[18] In his 2003 AERA presidential address, Linn ventured to project how long it might take us to get 100 percent of our students to proficient and how hard it might be. If we assume, said Linn, that we will continue to make the same progress on NAEP in the future as in the previous decade, we can get 100 percent of our students to reach proficient in mathematics in 61 years at the fourth grade, 66 years at the sixth grade, and 166 years at the twelfth grade.

Supposedly, though, NCLB will accelerate our improvement. Thus Linn asked by how much we must speed up if we wish to reach 100 percent proficiency by 2014. He found that we must accelerate the rate of improvement by a factor of four at grades 4 and 8 and a factor of twelve at grade 12 (see Figure 6–3). The reader is left to judge how doable this is. For his part, Linn called the mandate "quite unreasonable."[19]

As we have seen from the examples of California and Minnesota, even using state-developed tests, not NAEP, produces enormous quantities of school failures. Thus many of the schools parents now see as good will be labeled as failing. NCLB thus drives a wedge between parents and their schools. At the 2004 AERA convention, Colorado researchers reported that in the Boulder Valley School District that surrounds the University of Colorado, there were a number of surprise "failures" and that these failures caused parents a great deal of "dissonance."[20] The parents thought the schools were good, but NCLB said they were failing. That's the idea.

In order to get middle-class parents to consider vouchers, EMOs, or other instruments of privatization, those parents must

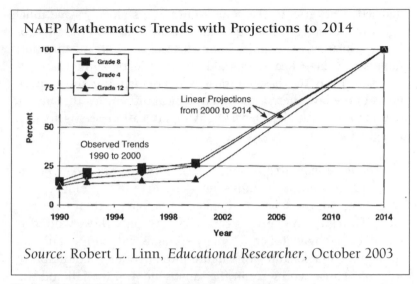

Figure 6–3. NAEP Mathematics Trends

be led to distrust their schools. NCLB is the perfect infernal machine for inculcating such distrust.

Schools that fail to make AYP are subject to increasingly severe penalties for each consecutive year they fail. One of the first penalties to kick in is the "choice option." Children in failing schools must be offered the opportunity to attend a successful school. The district must pay for transportation.

I note elsewhere in this book that 36 percent of our schools already utilize portables to ameliorate overcrowding. Transfers could well exacerbate such crowding. Doesn't matter. According to Eugene Hickok, Under Secretary of Education, the receiving school must "build capacity." It must bring in portables, build new classrooms, hire more teachers, whatever it takes. Only if the arriving students would so pack the schools as to violate fire or health codes can they be refused admission.

This should get interesting. Chicago reported in spring 2004 that it was obligated to offer the choice option to nearly 200,000 students but it had only 500 spaces for them.[21] Let us eagerly watch to see what Mr. Hickok does about this situation. In addition, because many failures will occur in urban areas, the choice option will collide with another provision of NCLB, the mandate for "highly qualified" teachers. As everyone knows, cities already have much higher proportions of underqualified teachers than do the suburbs. Where will they then find additional teachers with qualifications that meet the law? Readers should call Mr. Hickok and inquire.

Aside from the basic impossibility of meeting the requirements of the law, there are some technical difficulties that no one in Congress or at the Department of Education seems to have thought about:

1. *What about mobility?* In some urban schools, the kids who are there in May are not the kids who were there in September. How, then, can the *school* be held accountable for their performance? If a regulation appears that says "test only those who were in attendance by October 1," many students will simply fall through the cracks and won't figure into anyone's accountability program. Those who were in the same school in the fall and the spring might well constitute so small a group that it falls below the state's threshold for minimal group size for reporting data.

2. *What about summer loss?* Research finds that poor children gain about the same amount as their middle class and affluent peers during the school year, but while middle class and affluent children either hold their own or gain over the summer, poor children do not sustain what they learned in school. Thus, a number of schools that do an adequate job between September and June will be held accountable for what occurs in the months that they are closed.

3. *What about the impact of choice transfers on test scores?* Supposedly, the choice option goes first to the neediest children, that is, those with the lowest test scores. If a group of these hard-core nonachievers departs, that automatically raises the test score average of the sending school, perhaps getting it off the failed-schools list. At the same time, the receiving school must take on these children who have proven more difficult than most to educate. This could well transform a successful school into a failing one through no fault of the school's. And, incidentally, if the failing sending school does make AYP the next year, those who have transferred out do not have to return. Their parents, however, must then pay for transportation to the receiving school, turning NCLB into an unfunded mandate on mostly poor parents.

I was not alone in predicting high failure rates. In 2002, consultant and voucher advocate Denis Doyle wrote in his electronic newsletter, "the nation is about to be inundated in a sea of bad news" and that the public schools were going to get "poleaxed."[22] He sounded positively gleeful at the prospect.

Once the public schools got poleaxed, the door would be open to privatizers and vouchers. Privatizing the schools would give Bush three major victories.

1. It would establish a "healthy business climate" in education and would send much more money into the coffers of corporations as they take over the schools.

2. It would advance the agenda of the Business Roundtable, the principal organization advancing the high-standards, one-size-fits-all education for docility agenda represented by NCLB. (Ed Rust, CEO of State Farm Mutual and head of the BRT's education committee, was part of the Bush education transition team.)

3. It would destroy or at least greatly weaken the power of the National Education Association and the American Federation of Teachers whose five-or-so million members represent a large pool of Democratic voters.

Thus, while NCLB initially creates the impression that it runs counter to the Bush agenda, in fact, it advances that agenda in many ways.

So far, I'm happy to report, Doyle and I have both been wrong. It's hard to know what will happen if the Boulder Valley parents get year after year of "dissonance," but many parents appear to have at least initially rejected the "failing school" label. A February 2004 survey by the Opinion Research Company was headlined "Parent Support for No Child Left Behind Is Thin, Three Quarters Opposed Fund Cut-Off If Their Child's School 'Fails.'"[23] Note the quotes around "Fails," indicating that the parents don't buy it.

On the other hand, a June 2004 survey by ETS found that from 2001 to 2004 the percent of parents awarding schools an A dropped from 8 percent to 2 percent, and the percent of Bs declined from 35 percent to 20 percent. There were no results from SAT, NAEP, or international comparisons that could have produced this shift.

Voices against NCLB were heard in full force in early 2004. The Virginia House of Delegates, calling NCLB an unfunded mandate and an unwarranted federal intrusion, demanded an exemption from it. Although Republicans control the Virginia House, the measure passed 98–1 and a Democrat cast the lone No vote.[24] If one enters the words "No Child Left Behind" and "criticism" into a Google search, as of mid May, one obtained more than 24,000 results (some of which, it should be said, were defenses against the criticism). A few headlines: "Critics Say the 'No Child' Program Is a Setup for Public School Failure (*Salt Lake Tribune,* 23 February); "More States Are Fighting 'No Child Left Behind' Law" (*Washington Post,* 19 February); "An Education Rebellion Is Stirring" (*Christian Science Monitor,* 18 February); "States Fight No Child Left Behind, Calling It Intrusive" (*USA Today,* 11 February). On NPR's *Morning Edition,* host Bob Edwards called the criticism "ferocious," and education reporter Claudio Sanchez said the criticism erupted because states found the law "unfunded, unrealistic, and intrusive."[25]

Utah received considerable publicity when its House education panel recommended that Utah not participate. However, "Utah's shot across the bow at the No Child Left Behind Act went from that of a rifle to a pop gun" when the full House permitted districts to participate as long as federal monies fully covered the costs.[26] No state funds could be used. The Utah Senate, though, relegated the bill to "summer study."

According to Wisconsin Attorney General Peggy A. Lautenschlager, the state legislatures don't even need to get involved. In an eleven-page letter of constitutional analysis to State Senator Fred Risser, Lautenschlager pointed out that the Act itself restricts what federal agencies may require of states and localities:

§7907 **Prohibitions on Federal government and use of Federal Funds**
a. **General Prohibition** Nothing in this Act shall be construed to authorize an officer or employee of the Federal Government to mandate, direct, or control a State, local educational agency, or school's curriculum, program of instruction, or allocation of State or local resources, or mandate a State or any subdivision thereof to spend any funds or incur any costs not paid for under this act.[27]

In a visit to Milwaukee, Rod Paige said department lawyers were looking at Lautenschlager's analysis. "I'm very confident that the answer is going to be that the No Child Left Behind Act is sufficiently funded," he said.[28] Paige also repeated in Milwaukee something he has now come to say often: that NCLB requires children to perform at "grade level," not that it requires them to be "proficient."

One might wonder where, exactly, the criticism is coming from. Bruce Hunter, associate executive director of the American Association of School Administrators, thinks he can discern four discrete sources.

First come the state legislatures like Virginia that resent the federal intrusion. Hunter does allow that maybe this resentment would be tempered if the federal funds covered the expenses, but they don't. On the other hand, the resentment might be fueled because the federal government has never paid its proper share of special education costs. Estimates of how much NCLB will cost the states vary with assumptions made but the costs always exceed the federal funds, often by a great deal.[29]

Second would be members of AASA as well as other organizations who perceive NCLB to be based on a flawed strategy for organizational change—punishment. Indeed, punishment, as behaviorist B. F. Skinner never tired of telling us, doesn't have a great track record in any aspect of behavioral or institutional change.

Third are teachers and experts in various fields of instruction who perceive that the educational assumptions about learning embedded in NCLB are all wrong.

Finally, there are independent scholars, such as myself, Paul Barton, Bruce Biddle, David Berliner, Richard Kahlenberg, and Richard Rothstein, who in various publications have called attention to the role of social class and poverty in producing the "achievement gap." No Child Left Behind fails to address any of these issues save to target more Title I money to urban areas (but hardly enough to produce large improvements). I deal with poverty in Chapter 3 and the Biddle-Berliner analysis is discussed in Chapter 15. Barton lays out his thought in *Parsing the Achievement Gap*,[30] while Kahlenberg's monograph is *Can Separate Be Equal? The Overlooked Flaw at the Center of No Child Left Behind*.[31] Rothstein provides the most extensive treatment in *Class and Schools*.[32]

The criticism doesn't mean that the private sector isn't drooling over NCLB. The law does for the testing industry what Iraq did for Halliburton. And not just the testing industry. There are some $24.3 billion for companies to lust after in aid to high-poverty schools, reading programs, technology improvements, and building and running charter schools.[33]

> *The criticism doesn't mean that the private sector isn't drooling over NCLB. The law does for the testing industry what Iraq did for Halliburton.*

Some of the amounts charged are obscene. Kaplan, best known for its SAT-prep courses, will offer a half-day course to help teachers understand testing for three thousand dollars. If they can get teachers (or anyone not knowledgeable about tests) to "understand testing" in a half-day program, they'll earn every penny of it. My assessment course lasts fifteen weeks.

While AYP and the 2014 deadline have gotten most of the attention, the law's provisions for teachers pose vexing problems as well. All teachers in schools receiving NCLB funds must be "highly qualified" by the school year 2005–2006 as must be all teachers hired after the start of the 2002–2003 school year. By "highly qualified," NCLB means those who hold at least a bachelor's degree, have full state certification (or have passed the state's licensing exam), and have not had any certification requirements waived on "an emergency, provisional, or temporary basis."

In his second report titled *Meeting the Highly Qualified Teacher Challenge,* Secretary of Education Rod Paige outlined what he called in the report a "high standards, low barriers" approach to teacher certification. Relying on a quite sloppy analysis from the Abell Foundation,[34] Paige and the department hold that the important qualities a teacher must have are high verbal skills (usually defined as high SAT scores, but sometimes not defined at all) and content knowledge. Actually knowing how to teach children counts for very little.[35]

In working with this high standards, low barriers approach, the department has declared open season on colleges of education. At a conference, Bush reading czar Reid Lyon declared, "If there was any piece of legislation that I could pass, it would be to blow up colleges of education." Given that Paige called the National Education Association a terrorist organization, one wonders how much war metaphors pervade the Bush team's thinking about education (the video of Lyon's performance has been pulled from the website of the sponsoring agency, the Council for

Excellence in Government, but the story about his comments can still be found at *www.susanohanian.org/show_research.html?id=3*).

But then, as noted earlier, NCLB can readily be considered a preemptive strike against the public schools.

A Trend Spotted?

The No Child Left Behind Act was signed in January 2002. I completed my first critique the next month. No publication would touch it. When I tried to discuss my logic at the American Educational Research Association convention in April, I got a feeling similar to that described by Arlo Guthrie in his song/story "Alice's Restaurant." Sitting on a bench in a jail with others who had committed unspeakable crimes, Guthrie was asked what offense he had been charged with. "Littering," he replied. Then, he, said, "and they all moved away from me on the bench." Another early critic, Jamie McKenzie of Bellingham, Washington, reported a similar feeling: "I felt very much alone. Shunned. Avoided."[36]

At the 2003 convention, though, I had a number of people come up to me, individually, and say they now agreed with me, including three career staffers from the U.S. Department of Education (one of whom also said she was ashamed to be working for the department).

By 2004, opposing NCLB had gained enough legitimacy that the conference offered several sessions with titles like "NCLB: Educational Reform or Trojan Horse?" "NCLB: A Tragedy in One Act," and "NCLB: Were the First Year Outcomes as Dire as Predicted?" The answer to this last question was "yes," but that answer paled in light of failures-to-be in the coming years.

What will next year's convention bring?

Notes

1. Sanger, David E., and Jim Rutenberg. 2004. "Education Law Will Stand, Bush Tells Its Detractors." *New York Times,* 12 May, A18.

2. Welsh, John. 2004. "All Minnesota Left Behind?" *St. Paul Pioneer Press,* 26 February, A1.

3. Ivins, Molly. 2003. *Fresh Air.* 3 October. The program can be heard at *www.freshair.npr.org.*

4. Walsh-Sarnecki, Peggy. 2000. "Analysts Foresaw Defeat." *Detroit Free Press,* 9 November.

5. Wilgoren, Jodie. 2000. "Vouchers' Fare May Hinge on Name." *New York Times,* 20 December.

6. Hsu, Spencer. 2004. "Voucher Program Gets Final Approval." *Washington Post,* 22 January, A1.

7. "Ad Hoc Committee on Confirming Test Results." 2002. *Using the National Assessment of Educational Progress to Confirm State Test Results.* Washington, DC: National Assessment Governing Board.

8. Will, George F. 2003. "Shame: School Reform's Weak Weapon." *Washington Post,* 2 March, A27.

9. Princeton Review. 2003. *Testing the Testers: A Ranking of State Accountability Systems.* New York: Princeton Review.

10. U.S. General Accounting Office. 1993. *Education Achievement Standards: NAGB's Approach Yields Misleading Interpretations.* Washington, DC: General Accounting Office, Report No. GAO/PEMD-93-12.

11. National Academy of Education. 1997. *Assessment in Transition: Monitoring the Nation's Educational Progress.* Mountain View, CA: National Academy of Education.

12. National Academy of Sciences. 1999. *Grading the Nation's Report Card: Evaluating NAEP and Transforming the Assessment of Educational Progress.* Washington, DC: National Academy of Sciences.

13. Linn, Robert L. 1998. *Standards-Based Accountability: Ten Suggestions.* Los Angeles, CA: Center for Research in Evaluation, Student Standards and Testing, University of California, Los Angeles.

14. Jones, Lyle V. 1997. *National Tests and Educational Reform: Are They Compatible?* Princeton, NJ: Policy Information Center, Educational Testing Service.

15. U.S. Department of Education. 1999. *NAEP 1998 Reading Report Card for the Nation and the States.* Washington DC: U.S. Department of Education, Report No. NCES 1999-500.

16. U.S. Department of Education. 2003. *NAEP 2003 Reading Report Card for the Nation and the States.* Washington, DC: U.S. Department of Education.

17. U.S. Department of Education. 2003. *NAEP 2003 Mathematics*

Report Card for the National and the States. Washington, DC: U.S. Department of Education.

18. Linn, Robert L., Eva L. Baker, and Damian W. Betebenner. 2002. "Accountability Systems: Implications of Requirements of the No Child Left Behind Act of 2001. *Educational Researcher* (August/September): 3–16.

19. Linn, Robert L. 2003. "Accountability, Responsibility and Reasonable Expectations." *Educational Researcher* (October): 3–13.

20. Dings, Jonathan, and Carolyn Haug. 2004. "Impact of NCLB Adequate Yearly Progress on District Accountability in Colorado." Paper delivered to the annual convention of the American Educational Research Association, San Diego, California, April 12–16.

21. Rossi, Rosalind. 2004. "Student Transfers Face Tough Odds." *Chicago Sun-Times,* 20 April, A1.

22. Doyle, Denis P. 2002. "AYP Revealed, Now What?" *The Doyle Report,* 4 June. "AYP Once More Once." *The Doyle Report,* 13 June. Accessed at *www.thedoylereport.com.*

23. Opinion Research Company. 2004. "Parent Support for No Child Left Behind Is Thin, Three-Quarters Oppose Funds Cut-Off If Their Child's School 'Fails.'" *www.resultsforamerica.org.* Click on Results in Education.

24. Becker, Jo, and Rosalind S. Helderman. 2004. "Va. Seeks to Leave Bush Law Behind." *Washington Post,* 24 January, A1.

25. National Public Radio. 2004. "'No Child Left Behind' Criticism Widespread." *Morning Edition,* 19 April.

26. Toomer-Cook, Jennifer. 2004. "No to Unfunded 'No Child' Act." *Deseret Morning News,* 11 February.

27. Lautenschlager, Peggy A. 2004. Opinion delivered to State Senator Fred Risser, 12 May.

28. Borsuk, Alan J. 2004. "Paige Make Case for Left Behind Law: He Says Program Adequately Funded." *Milwaukee Journal-Sentinel,* 24 May.

29. Mathis, William J. 2003. "No Child Left Behind: Costs and Benefits." *Phi Delta Kappan* (May): 679–86.

30. Barton, Paul. 2004. *Parsing the Achievement Gap.* Princeton, NJ: Policy Information Center, Educational Testing Service.

31. Kahlenberg, Richard T. 2004. *Can Separate Be Equal? The Overlooked Flaw at the Center of No Child Left Behind.* New York: Century Foundation.

32. Rothstein, Richard. 2004. *Class and Schools: Using Social, Economic, and Educational Reform to Close the Black-White Achievement Gap.* Washington, DC: Economic Policy Institute.

33. Kronholz, June. 2003. "Education Firms See Money in Bush's School-Boost." *Wall Street Journal,* 24 December, A1.

34. Walsh, Kate. 2001. *Teacher Certification Reconsidered: Stumbling Towards Quality* (November). Baltimore, MD: Abell Foundation.

35. U.S. Department of Education. 2003. *Meeting the Highly Qualified Teacher Challenge.* Washington, DC: U.S. Department of Education.

36. McKenzie, Jamie. 2004. Personal communication (e-mail), 18 May.

7 Handing Over Schools to Business

What do I say when people say, "Schools won't improve until they're taken over by private companies and run like businesses"?

You can say, "So far, the businesses that have taken over schools haven't managed to get achievement up and they're mostly losing money as well." If you're feeling sassy, you can begin your rebuttal with "Oh, like Enron, Imclone, and WorldCom?"

Venture capitalists called the private companies that run public schools educational management organizations (EMOs) and they drew the analogy to health management organizations (HMOs). Given the state of managed care in this country, that alone should serve to alarm.

The first EMO to garner much press or attention from Wall Street was TesseracT, née Educational Alternatives, Inc., or EAI. In the early 1990s, under the aggressive leadership of CEO John Golle, EAI landed contracts to manage schools in Hartford, Connecticut, Dade County, Florida, and Baltimore, Maryland. Early on, EAI employed some of the creative accounting methods that would later do in many larger corporations. In its contract with Baltimore, for example, most of the money was required to cover teacher salaries, but EAI's books showed this money as unrestricted income. It also invested substantial amounts in high-risk derivatives and much of its "profit" was actually interest from these investments.

After touting large test-score gains, EAI had to admit that the figure it publicized was an error. Baltimore hired the University of Maryland, Baltimore County (UMBC) to conduct an external evaluation. UMBC was unable to find any test score gains in the nine EAI schools.[1]

To save money, EAI dismissed most of the paraprofessionals in its schools, replacing them with low-wage interns. The paraprofessionals had mostly lived in the schools' neighborhoods. The interns did not. Thus a substantial sum of money moved from the blighted areas of the schools to elsewhere.

Another evaluation, this one by the Washington, D.C.–based Economic Policy Institute, found that EAI's books were something of a mystery and that whatever profit it might have turned came from interest on investments and speculation on EAI stock. "EAI has yet to show that it can make a profit by managing schools."[2]

All three of the East Coast contracts ended on less than friendly terms. Golle then changed the name, the headquarters' location, and the mission of EAI. It became the TesseracT Group (after Madeleine L'Engle's *A Wrinkle in Time*), moved to the toney Phoenix suburb of Scottsdale, and began opening private schools for which it charged up to eight thousand dollars a year in tuition. It also purchased twenty-two preschools and some charter schools.

As in Baltimore, a fair share of TesseracT's income in Arizona did not stem from the astute management of schools. It came from charging the state $1.95 a mile for transporting students to and from charters and reimbursing parents only five cents a mile. In one three-month period, it made $760,000 through such charges. The Arizona legislature then closed the loophole that permitted such outrageous profiteering, limiting reimbursement to $174 per pupil per year.[3]

Although in 1999 Golle was still in an expansive mode, he was expanding too rapidly, and TesseracT found itself with cash-flow problems. Shareholders rejected a plan to acquire five million dollars in return for permitting the loaner to convert unpaid principal to TesseracT shares. This turned out to be good luck for the would-be loan maker, as TesseracT shares, which had peaked at $48.50 on the NASDAQ, plummeted to 56 cents a share. NASDAQ delisted the stock.

"The worst is behind us," said Golle, as 2000 dawned.[4] It was not. By May 2000, TesseracT's debt totaled 48.9 million dollars and it was hemorrhaging 12 million dollars a year. To stanch the flow, it closed some schools. Some high-level executives resigned, no reasons given.[5]

By the start of the 2000–2001 school year, TesseracT had trimmed its administrative staff by 80 percent. On October 9, 2000, Columbus day observed, a school holiday, TesseracT filed Chapter 11 Bankruptcy. It never emerged. It sold its private schools to parent groups that had formed corporations in order to acquire them, and sold its preschools to Sunrise Preschools.

The best known of the remaining EMOs is Edison Schools, but there are others: the Leona Group, Beacon Management, Mosaica, Chancellor Academies, White Hat Management, National Heritage Academies, and so on. An annual report tracking such companies by Alex Molnar, Glen Wilson, and Daniel Allen of Arizona State University indicated that there are fifty-one companies managing 463 schools in twenty-eight states and the District of Columbia.[6] Most of the managed schools—373—are in the hands of the thirteen companies that manage more than 10 schools each (using conventional school-counting techniques, the Arizona State team shows Edison with 109). Thirty companies manage only 1 school. Altogether, the managed schools contain 200,403 students.

We can get some idea of the difficulties business firms encounter when trying to run schools like businesses by reviewing the history of Edison Schools, Inc., founded by H. Christopher Whittle. Whittle announced the creation of Edison with great hoopla in 1991. He has sought—and received—much media attention in the ensuing years, from both the education and the business press. So we turn to a detailed account of its rise and, if not fall, slump.

Announced as the Edison Project in 1991, Edison Schools promised a revolution in education—for free. Whittle promised Edison schools would cost no more than regular schools. Edison has delivered neither the revolution in schooling nor the low costs. Edison schools invariably cost more. Edison truly gave the game away when it negotiated its largest contract, for twenty schools in Philadelphia. It asked for fifteen hundred dollars per pupil above the amount allotted per student for public schools. It got only eight hundred dollars. Dallas reported that Edison schools there cost the district two thousand dollars per pupil per year more than regular schools, one reason that Dallas terminated the contract (mediocre performance was another).

Whittle promised computers in the homes of pupils as well as in the schools, all connected to the Internet. Students would learn to read from classic books, not basals. Edison would offer a project-based science curriculum and would send the students' projects via Internet to experts all over the country who would evaluate them. By the time students left Edison schools, *all* of them would have taken either calculus or a college-level course in probability and statistics (currently, about 7 percent of students nationally take calculus in high school).

And all of this would be free—it would cost no more than the per pupil expenditures of public schools.

Whittle has on more than one occasion been likened to Harold Hill, scam artist of *The Music Man*. He tends toward hyperbole, but has a great deal of charisma to go along with it. His success in the business world has been mixed. He and a college chum, Philip Moffitt, made considerable amounts of money publishing guides to college towns, most notably Knoxville, Tennessee, home to their alma mater, the University of Tennessee. With these profits in hand, they bought *Esquire* magazine in 1979. At the time, *Esquire* was in such dire straits that no one gave them a chance for success, but they did in fact turn it around and five years later celebrated the magazine's fiftieth anniversary with a black-tie affair for which they rented Avery Fisher Hall at Lincoln Center. Whittle bought a townhouse on Manhattan's East Side and a $7.9 million estate in East Hampton. (In 2002, he put the estate on the market at $45 million and reputedly sold it to clothing magnate Tommy Hilfiger for $31 million. The deal was announced in a variety of publications, including *Forbes,* then denied. If true, the drop from $45 million to $31 million would still leave Whittle with a tidy profit—given his $7.9 million purchase price in 1989.[7]) In 1986, they sold *Esquire* to Hearst and split. The introspective, yoga-practicing Moffitt took up Jungian psychology while the exuberant Whittle set sail searching for bigger ventures in communications.

One project, Medical News Network, consumed $100 million in start-up costs and never recovered. Another operation, Special Projects, sent information and ads into doctors' offices and waiting rooms. It was initially profitable but then sputtered. Channel One beamed news—and ads—into classrooms. Channel One enjoyed some success, especially in the South and Midwest, but was blocked by the Regents in New York and functionally blocked by the courts in California—the judge permitted schools to show

Channel One but struck that part of the contract which forced all teachers to show it and all students to watch. When districts in Texas, Channel One's biggest client, defected in droves as their three-year contracts expired, Whittle sold the company to KIII Communications and concentrated on Edison.

In 1991, he announced that he would have two hundred private schools by 1996, one thousand by the end of the century. He estimated that it would take $2.5 billion to fulfill his vision. Alas for Whittle, this vision depended on George H. W. Bush winning a second term in 1992. In 1991, after the Gulf War I, that looked certain. Bush's secretary of education at the time was Lamar Alexander, who had been a paid consultant to Whittle and also served on Whittle Communications' board of directors. Alexander had purchased $10,000 of Whittle Communications stock. Whittle later bought it back for $330,000.

Though he never said so publicly, to realize his vision, Whittle needed Bush and Alexander to push voucher legislation through Congress. It was the only way he could possibly create clients for his schools: the middle class had no desire to leave their good schools, and without help, the poor couldn't afford tuition for Whittle's new institutions. Vouchers would let them try the new schools for free. But the unthinkable happened and Bush lost to antivoucher Clinton. Whittle had to settle for managing, not owning, a few schools, and as Edison grew, they became increasingly located in poor city neighborhoods.

Whittle took the company public in 1999. He hoped the IPO would come in at $25 a share, but it mustered only $18. The stock did rise as high as $39 and while it was up, Whittle cashed in some of his stock options for $16 million. The timing of his sale, early 2001, turned out to be propitious.

In the spring of 2001, Harold Levy, then chancellor of New York City's public schools, wanted Edison to manage five of his lowest-performing schools. He couldn't just *give* the contract to Whittle, but his criteria for bidders excluded everyone but Edison. Levy's plan, though, contained a fatal flaw: parents had to vote on the idea. At first, Levy permitted only Edison to distribute information about the vote, but community groups' outrage forced him to allow them to distribute anti-Edison leaflets.

The parents voted 4 to 1 against Edison. Edison's stock drifted down to $12 a share. Edison remained in the red.

In the summer of 2001, Tom Ridge, at the time governor of Pennsylvania, presented Edison with a much larger opportunity than Levy had in New York. Ridge had been threatening a state takeover of the Philadelphia school district for years. He had delayed because he was among those being considered to run on the Republican ticket with George W. Bush in 2000. A takeover, with its attendant negativity and discordant media stories, could lower his chances.

When Bush tapped Dick Cheney, he freed Ridge to pursue the takeover. In July 2001, he awarded Edison a $2.7 million no-bid (and probably illegal) contract to "study" the Philadelphia school district. In only two months, Edison spent all of the money and completed its report. It was an amazing performance. Most universities or think tanks would have taken several years for such a project. Indeed, the RAND Corporation's evaluation of Edison has thus far taken four years.

The Council of the Great City Schools analyzed the Edison report and concluded it used "weak techniques and questionable assumptions" to reach its conclusions and that those conclusions "appear[ed] to have been reached before any data were analyzed or any interviews conducted."[8] Questions on attitude surveys were phrased to ensure that the district looked bad.

Edison, to no one's surprise, recommended that forty-five administrators be replaced by Edison appointees and that Edison directly manage forty-five schools. The resulting contract would be worth $300 million over three years. Whittle had claimed that Edison might be profitable in 1998 and surely would be in 1999, but in the summer of 2001, it had yet to see a quarter in the black. The Philadelphia contract would surely cure that problem.

Edison, to no one's surprise, recommended that forty-five administrators be replaced by Edison appointees and that Edison directly manage forty-five schools. The resulting contract would be worth $300 million over three years.

If white Republican governor Ridge wanted Edison, African American Democratic Philadelphia mayor John Street did not. After much bickering, though, they managed to plaster on smiles at a press conference where they announced the joint appointment of a School Reform Commission (SRC) to oversee the changes in Philadelphia. The SRC showed much more independence than anyone expected and awarded contracts to a variety of vendors. It gave Edison only twenty schools. Although that was twice as many schools as in any other Edison contract, Edison had asked for forty-five and, coming after the debacle in New York, investors took the twenty schools as signifying the SRC had no confidence in the company. Edison stock sank below a dollar. To stave off delisting by the NASDAQ stock exchange, Edison desperately bought back shares. This lifted the stock from $0.14 a share to as high as $1.75.

Edison has grown, mostly from Whittle's tireless salesman-ship, but many of Edison's early customers have left. The Edison record of nonachievement is one major reason. Schools that Edison touts as showing "positive" test score trends have been demoted to "unacceptable" by Texas and California, two states with state school ranking systems. One "positive" school in San Francisco finished dead last among the seventy-five elementary schools in that city.

The curriculum revolution Whittle promised in 1991 has never materialized. Edison uses off-the-shelf curricula developed by regular educators, the reading program from Success for All, and Everyday Mathematics, developed at the University of Chicago. Those programs are fairly well regarded but they are hardly the innovative curricula Whittle promised. Worse, evaluations of Edison schools find mixed results at best.

The curriculum revolution Whittle promised in 1991 has never materialized.

Edison is fond of saying that 84 percent of its schools show positive trends. Edison's way of calculating a trend, though, gives it every advantage. When *New York Times* reporters Jacques Steinberg and Diana Henriques applied Edison's technique to Cleveland's public schools, 87 percent of them showed positive trends.[9] No one holds up Cleveland schools as models for emulation. Cleveland officials said they were "very worried" about some of the "positive" schools that turned up in Steinberg and Henriques' analysis.

Researchers at Western Michigan University also found that many of the schools that Edison's reports claimed had positive trends were actually mixed. Edison does not take kindly to such findings. Chief Education Officer John Chubb called it "stunningly irresponsible." He continued, "The Western Michigan report is literally a scam . . . It is shocking that social scientists would attempt to pass off such work as an objective evaluation."[10]

That Edison's students' achievement is so mediocre is surprising given some aspects of Edison schools. Edison schools run a longer school day and a longer school year. Edison students attend 50 percent more hours a year than students in regular schools.[11] They also spend ninety minutes a day each on reading and math. Certainly there is no one-to-one correspondence between time in class and achievement, but one would expect so many extra hours to produce *some* improvement.

Not only has Edison rejected specific evaluations of its schools, but its *Fourth Annual Report on Student Performance* rejected the most common *type* of evaluation: the comparison of Edison schools to demographically similar schools, comparisons that are the essence of the evaluation systems in California and Texas. Edison claims that its schools serve as models for the district and the other schools are not, therefore, independent of Edison. Interestingly, the report holds up schools in Wichita as such models. Shortly after the report appeared, Wichita terminated its contract with Edison. Some models.[12]

Edison also claims that Edison schools, being schools of choice, show marked changes in their demographics once Edison arrives. It therefore rejects before-Edison and after-Edison comparisons. People differ on why Edison schools change with time. Some have accused them of "counseling out" low-scoring children and those in need of special education services. Initially Edison did say that it would provide only those special education services that could be administered by the regular classroom teachers. It later changed policy and hired special education teachers who move from classroom to classroom. Edison schools generally have few, sometimes very few, children receiving special education or English Language Learners.

Edison does not apparently realize that by rejecting before-and-after evaluations it also logically knocks out as well the one evaluation it does recognize: evaluation over time after Edison's arrival. Edison's demographic changes do not happen all at once. They happen over a period of years. If the demographics are in flux, then this type of evaluation is just as invalid as the before-

and-after-Edison comparison. Edison's method would be valid if Edison tracked the *same students* over time, but this is something Edison does not do. (Under those conditions, before-and-after Edison comparisons would also be valid.)

In November 2003, Whittle took the company private again. The Florida Retirement System bought it via its investment firm, Liberty Partners. About 50 percent of FRS members are retired public school teachers. Imagine. Public school teachers entrusting their money to a company dedicated to destroying public schools. Well, the teachers didn't actually do it. The Florida State Board of Administration, of which Governor Jeb Bush is one-third, did it. The people who suffer the results of any action of the FRS have absolutely no voice in what it does.

Some feel that Liberty took this action to please Bush. Its contract was up for renewal and it had been the victim of scathing analyses about the quality of its operation. An Edison collapse would be not merely a business failure, but an enormous embarrassment to those advocating privatization, and Jeb Bush is one such. How better to please the governor than to save the poster child of privatization?

As it happened, the purchase took place on July 14, 2003. On July 15, an officer in the Florida State Board of Administration proposed changes in Liberty's contract that would have prevented the purchase. How convenient. Liberty also hired a Philadelphia law firm to review the Edison deal. Said law firm had also reviewed the contract Edison had proposed in Philadelphia. James Cayne, chairman of Bear Stearns, also provides a political link to the purchase. He had found Liberty as the buyer of Edison, is also a "Pioneer," the designation given to the second-highest level of donors to George W. Bush.[13] The convenience and coincidence appear to know no bounds.

As usual, whatever slings and arrows of outrageous fortune others suffer, Whittle lands on his feet. Indeed, a 2003 *Fortune* article was titled "The Nine Lives of Chris Whittle.[14] He retains 4 percent of the shares and his salary rises from $345,000 to $600,000 a year with potential bonuses upping that by 275 percent.[15] When one examines the logic of this deal, one is prompted to ask, "Excuse me, was all the Enron stock spoken for?"

The *Orlando Business Journal* analyzed the transaction in a Harper's Index by-the-numbers fashion, which follows:

$2,175,000—the amount of money Edison loaned Whittle to buy Edison stock.

$5,694,000—the amount of money Edison loaned Whittle to pay for taxes on stock purchases.

24 and 29—the number of Edison contracts that expire in 2003–2004 and 2004–2005.

16.2 and 22.4—the percent of Edison net revenue represented by those contracts.

2—the number of brain cells, which, when rubbed together, generate sufficient spark to assess, consider—and toss—this dog of a deal.[16]

> *If Edison is the model of privatization of public schools, public school officials can rest easy.*

If Edison is the model of privatization of public schools, public school officials can rest easy.

I cannot not leave this subject without alerting readers to another corporation that is developing a huge system of privatized delivery of educational services, a corporation run by people with a track record of making grand sums of money and turning profits. The corporation is called Knowledge Universe (KU) and it might be called the anti-Edison, analogous to antimatter. While Edison announced the formation of the company with great public hoopla and issued press releases to document every new contract or to advertise the "successes" described in the annual reports, KU keeps mum.

KU was started in 1996 by former junk bond king Michael Milken, his brother Lowell, and Larry Ellison, founder of Oracle Corporation. Although it is often described as octopuslike, no one fully knows the size or reach of KU because it is a privately held company. If you go to KU's website (*www.knowledgeu.com*), you won't find a "contact us" button. You won't find a "search the site" option or a site map. If you go to the press room, you will find phone, fax, and e-mail information but you will be advised that "these contacts are reserved exclusively for accredited media representatives. . . . We'll need to know your name, publication, phone number, e-mail address, and deadline."

I called anyway and explained that I was writing a paper on

virtual schools for a policy group at Arizona State University. I was interested in talking with someone about K12, former Secretary of Education William Bennett's online for-profit virtual school project, in which KU has invested $10 million. I experienced a chilly reception and extensive and skeptical questioning. The person on the other end, never identified, took my phone number and e-mail address. Shortly thereafter, an e-mail arrived from a Robin Sherman, not further identified:

> I've been asked to advise you to contact the individual companies directly as our website shows only samples of investments. As a private company, we do not publish a full list of companies and the companies change from time to time as investments change. www.K12.com has contact information for K12. Please contact them directly.

Well.

From its holdings in some public companies and from activities recorded by business media, we can determine a few things about KU. In addition to partial ownership of K12, KU has a 16 percent control over Nobel Learning Communities, a publicly traded corporation that builds and operates private schools for upwardly mobile families who can't yet afford the cost of the established, elite privates. It owns outright about four hundred preschools. It has a graduate program offering an MBA at something called Cardean University, which actually offers a curriculum developed by the faculties at Stanford, Carnegie Mellon, Columbia, the University of Chicago, and the London School of Economics.

How an ex-felon like Milken managed to get affiliated with such prestigious universities without their knowing it is an interesting story. My take on KU and on its investment in K12, can be found at *www.asu.edu/educ/epsl/EPRU/documents/EPSL-0404-118-EPRU.doc*.[17]

KU owns a variety of businesses that offer various training and professional development services to people in the workforce and one online, school-related operation starts with children and runs through grandparenthood, offering advice and activities for interacting with children.

Without question, the most successful KU business is LeapFrog, a once small maker of learn-to-read toys, now the third largest toy maker in the country behind Mattel and Hasbro and also the fastest growing. (Thomas Kalinske, KU's CEO, was earlier CEO at Mattel, where he resuscitated Barbie dolls, and at Sega America, where he introduced Sonic the Hedgehog.) In 2002, LeapFrog's principal product, LeapPad, was the best-selling toy in America.

Without question, the most insidious-sounding business in the KU galaxy is Hypnotic. Hypnotic wants to build a better branding iron to brand people to products:

> To brand beyond the current cluttered world of advertising and establish a deeper emotional connection with consumers, brand marketers are beginning to deploy a new form of marketing communication, Branded Entertainment. The most successful of these unique and cost-efficient marketing programs account for a new technology, take advantage of integrated marketing initiatives and capture the hypnotic effect of pop-culture.[18]

"Deeper emotional connection"? You are getting sleepy . . . sleepy.

As far as I know, KU is not yet in the prenatal, perinatal, and undergraduate markets, but that might be coming, or it might be here but secret. The idea is clearly to have a constellation of operations that provide cradle-to-grave services. Kids will play with KU toys and see them on television (KU has access to all of the characters from the Learning Company). As students, they will use KU curricula and receive test-taking training from KU online test-prep companies. As workers, they will learn new skills and receive additional development from KU service providers (a guiding KU assumption is that in the "new" economy, workers must constantly update old skills and learn new ones). KU companies will provide after-school activities (they already do) and help parents and grandparents interact with children. One wonders how far Hypnotic's "Branded Entertainment" can be extended.

So how come you don't know about KU? Most educators, if they know about Michael Milken at all other than as the former junk bond king, know him as someone who shows up at school assemblies, flashes a broad smile, and hands out one hundred checks a year for $25,000 each to surprised teachers. According to one observer, "Thanks in part to Milken's fanatical secrecy, his flurry of acquisitions has received remarkably little attention.

Even Benno Schmidt [CEO] of the Edison Project pleads inno-
cent of the Milken for-profit operations."[19] Another chronicler
wrote, "Lastly, in a category all its own, there's Knowledge
Universe, the secretive two-year-old behemoth created by junk-
bond king, Michael Milken, his brother Lowell and Larry Ellison.
If you haven't heard much about them, you will."[20] Six years after
those words were written, most educators still haven't. But they
will.

Notes

1. Williams, Lois C., and Lawrence Leak. 1995. *The UMBC Evaluation
of the EAI Program in Baltimore County.* Baltimore: Center for
Educational Research, University of Maryland, Baltimore County.

2. Richards, Craig E., Rima Shore, and Max A. Sawicky. 1996. *Risky
Business: The Private Management of Public Schools,* 85. Washington,
DC: Economic Policy Institute.

3. Mattern, Hal. 2000a. "TesseracT Crisis Watched as Bellwether for
Private Schools." *Arizona Republic,* 20 February, A1.

4. Ibid.

5. Mattern, Hal. 2000b. "TesseracT Nears $50 Million Deficit Mark."
Arizona Republic, 23 May, D1.

6. Molnar, Alex, Glen Wilson, and Daniel Allen. 2004. *Profiles of For-
Profit Education Management Companies: Sixth Annual Report,
2003–2004.* Tempe, AZ: Arizona State University. *www.asu.edu/educ/epsl
/CERU/Documents/EPSL-0402-101-CERU.pdf.*

7. Schiffman, Betsy. 2002. "Movers and Shakers." *Forbes* (15
November).

8. Council of Great City Schools. 2001. *Strengthening the Performance
of the Philadelphia School District: Analysis and Comment on the Edison
Report.* Washington, DC: Council of the Great City Schools.

9. Steinberg, Jacques, and Diana B. Henriques. 2002. "Complex
Calculations on Academics." *New York Times,* 16 July, A10.

10. Edison Schools. 2001. "Union-Sponsored Study Proves Predictably
Biased Evaluation of Schools." *PR Newswire,* 22 February.

11. This would not be true in those areas, mostly cities, that have
added to the traditional 180-day year in order to lift the achievement
of low-scoring children.

12. Edison Schools. 2002. *Fourth Annual Report on Student Performance*. New York: Edison Schools.

13. Moberg, David. 2004. "How Edison Survived." *The Nation*, 15 March.

14. Schwartz, Nelson D. 2003. "The Nine Lives of Chris Whittle." *Fortune* (October).

15. Hurst, Marianne D. 2003. "Teachers Riled by Edison Deal." *Education Week* (8 October): 1.

16. "Counting Change." 2003. Editorial. *Orlando Business Journal*, 10 November.

17. Bracey, Gerald W. 2004. "Knowledge Universe and Virtual Schools: Educational Breakthrough or Digital Raid on the Public Treasury?" *www.asu.edu/educ/epsl/EPRU/documents/EPSL-0404-118-EPRU.doc*

18. Quote taken from *www.hypnotic.com/profile.aspx*.

19. Baker, Russ. 1999. "The Education of Mike Milliken." *The Nation*, 15 April.

20. Savitz, Eric J. 1998. "For Adults Only." *Barron's*, 2 March, 31.

Charter Schools Go Off Course

What do I say when someone says, "Let's make all schools charter schools and they'll be laboratories of innovation to transform the whole system"?

You can say, "A few charters might be laboratories of innovation, but mostly charter schools look like the schools they were supposed to replace. They don't outperform public schools and, in fact, often score lower on tests than demographically similar public schools. People were outraged by the supposedly poor performance of public schools. They should be equally outraged at the even lower achievement of charters. Some charters with low test scores have pulled a classic bait and switch. Having promised to raise achievement and failed, they now declare that achievement is irrelevant."

Charter schools represent a simple idea. You can substitute *contract* for *charter* with no loss of meaning. The person who invented the term *charter*, a Massachusetts teacher named Ray Budde, now retired, had in mind something like the charter between Henry Hudson and the directors of the East India Company in 1609. The charter spelled out precisely what Hudson would do, how he would be rewarded for it, and how he would be held accountable. Budde formed his notions in the 1970s but it wasn't until Albert Shanker, then president of the American Federation of Teachers, championed the concept ten years later that it became popularized. (Shanker and the AFT later pronounced themselves disillusioned by what had happened to the charter concept; in 2003, the AFT called for a moratorium on new charters until the existing ones provided more convincing evidence about their achievement.[1])

Early charter enthusiasts presented an equally simple idea for the rules by which charters would operate. In 1996, Joe Nathan, an advocate at the University of Minnesota, penned what was a common stance: "Hundreds of charter schools have been created around this nation by educators who are willing to put their jobs on the line to say 'If we can't improve students' achievement, close down our school.' That is accountability—clear, specific and real."[2] And pretty much nonexistent. Let us call this the Nathan Criterion: improve or die.

In 2001, the idea that charters would substitute accountability by performance instead of the traditional accountability by compliance with rules and regulations was still prominent:

> Conventional public schools are considered accountable because they must follow all the rules set by local and state school boards, and abide by all the provisions of contracts that these boards enter with unions and other organizations. Charter schools are exempted from many of these rules, and instead are required to demonstrate student learning.[3]

States and chartering authorities have not acted on the Nathan Criterion. In the same year that Nathan was effusing over charters, three other supporters wrote that they "had yet to see a single state with a thoughtful and well-formed plan for evaluating its charter school program."[4] Three years later, one of them, Bruno Manno, returned to report no progress:

> Today it's hard to know how well charter schools are actually doing . . . There are three predominant reasons for this situation.
> First, the charter strategy is so new that it's difficult to measure results. There's just not much data out. Second, today's charter accountability systems remain underdeveloped, often clumsy and ill fitting and are themselves beset by dilemmas. A final reason for the dearth of good accountability information lies with the charter authorizers and operators. Truth be told, they are often content to leave accountability agreements nebulous and undefined.[5]

As in all other human endeavors, the desire to look good trumps the need to be accountable.

Manno did not appear to realize that his final reason is in large part the cause of the first reason. There's not much data out there because people don't want to collect it. As in all other human endeavors, the desire to look good trumps the need to be accountable. In the dispassionate words of Jeffrey Henig at George Washington University, "charter schools show few signs of interest in systematic empirical research that is ultimately needed if we are going to be able to separate bold claim from proven perform-ance. Premature claims of success, reliance on anecdotal and unreliable evidence are still the rule of the day."[6] Ten years on, they still are. Nathan's hundreds of educators who put their jobs on the line are nowhere to be found. Truth loses out to advertis-ing. Image triumphs over substance.

In fact, only a small percentage of charter schools have been closed, usually for fiscal mismanagement, not failing achieve-ment. Katrina Bulkley of Rutgers described what she terms the "accountability bind" when it comes to evaluating and possibly closing a charter school:

1. Educational performance is not simple to define or measure, nor is how good is "good enough" in educational quality (although the Bush administration's emphasis on test scores have certainly pushed the country towards simplistic evalua-tions). In this context, charter authorizers sometimes turn to "proxies" to assess school quality.

2. Other aspects of a school's program, often more difficult to measure than test scores, are also important for families and authorizers.

3. Teachers, parents and students become very vested in particu-lar schools and destroying the community represented by the schools is more difficult than serving a diffuse public interest such as accountability.

4. Charter schools have become a highly politicized issue. Some authorizers fear that deciding to close a school might reflect poorly on the whole concept of charter schools as a means of reform.[7]

"Laboratories of innovation" is virtually a mantra for charters. If one searches on the terms *laboratories of innovation* and *charter schools* in Google, one obtains nearly 3,500 results. Part of the problem with charters is that many of those who actually would create something like a laboratory of innovation have a vision of education and little more. Suddenly they find they need expertise in fiscal and personnel matters, competence in budgeting, admin-istration, and, especially, fund-raising. In one instance, the simple requirement that teachers be fingerprinted, something routinely handled in public schools, apparently baffled a group who wished to start a charter school. A reporter wrote, "school officials acknowledged that they had little experience running a school and were stumped by the obstacles they faced."[8] The obstacles, in this case, did not include a hostile local school district or board.

When one examines the performance of charter schools today, one is hard-pressed to understand what the excitement was about. Researchers in the three most charter-active states, Arizona, California, and Michigan, have conducted evaluations. In another active state, Ohio, the state legislature set up the Legislative Office of Education Oversight, which is charged with the evaluation of charter schools. To a review of these four states we now turn.

> *When one examines the performance of charter schools today, one is hard-pressed to understand what the excitement was about.*

Arizona

One wouldn't expect much in accountability in Arizona, where, according to one legislator, "Anyone who could stand up and breathe got a charter."[9] In addition to handing out charters in Wild West fashion, the state superintendent of education, Lisa Keegan, refused to conduct evaluations (Keegan had, earlier, as a state legislator, authored Arizona's charter law). When the state department of education investigated charter schools, Keegan withheld the report for a year and killed the charter-monitoring program. She transferred the head of the program to another position (the transferee subsequently entered the private sector).

Before Keegan killed the monitoring program, the team had found that many courses in charter high schools lasted only a few weeks and rarely assigned homework. Some courses were at the seventh- or eighth-grade level. Some schools ran two or three four-hour shifts a day—Arizona law requires high school students attend only four hours a day. When Thomas Toch, then a reporter for *U.S. News and World Report,* visited one charter school, he dropped in on a course called American Literature Through Cinema. The class was studying *The Last of the Mohicans* at the time. But the kids were not watching Daniel Day-Lewis dashing through the woods. They were only listening to the sound track—except, observed Toch, those who were asleep.[10]

One evaluation in Arizona found that the percentage of white students in charter schools was increasing and that the percentage of white students in charter schools was much higher than the percentage of white students in the physically closest public school.[11] Anecdotal evidence has it that charters are becoming, in this the fiftieth anniversary of *Brown v. Board of Education*, increasingly homogeneous.[12] These anecdotes are confirmed in a formal study from the Civil Rights Project at Harvard.[13]

A statewide evaluation by the Center for Market-Based Education at the Goldwater Institute in Phoenix claimed that students who attended charter schools for two or three consecutive years gained more on tests than students in traditional public schools in the same period, although their scores remained below those in public schools.[14] This research is an econometric study. Because econometric studies are notoriously opaque and because econometrics is not my forte, I sent the report to several economists for comment. The typical comment was "It's a little hard to tell what they actually did. The descriptions of their research methods are poor."

Researchers at Michigan's W. E. Upjohn Institute for Employment Research criticized the study on several methodological grounds.[15] Their report is also filled with conditional clauses such as "As we understand it" and "it appears as if," indicating that they, too, have doubts about what the Goldwater team actually did.

The study also found that students who started in a traditional public school and then moved to a charter lost ground. Students who started in a charter and then moved to a traditional school gained ground. The researchers speculated that perhaps the year in a charter had given the students sufficient academic grounding for further learning. This seems like a stretch. The differences were only two or three percentile ranks, hardly good evidence for solid "grounding."

All interpretations of charter school evaluations are complicated by the fact that charter schools are typically small and have small classes. Both small schools and small class size have been shown to improve achievement, so any increasing achievement might be due to some size factor rather than some quality of the charter school itself. Unfortunately, no study has tried to partial out any effect of school or class size.

California

Several evaluations of charters have been conducted in California. One by Amy Stuart Wells at UCLA (now at Columbia University) is of particular interest because she and her team evaluated charters in terms of testing claims made for charter schools:

1. *Accountability.* Because charter schools are more accountable for student outcomes, charters will increase efforts to meet their goals.
2. *Efficiency.* Freed from the shackles of public school bureaucracies, charter schools will be more efficient and/or will be able to accomplish more with fewer resources.
3. *Competition.* By creating competition for other schools in the district, charters will force change in the public schools.
4. *Innovation.* Charters will create new models of schooling from which public schools can learn or which they can adopt.
5. *Choice.* Because charter schools will be developing new models of schooling, their presence will offer parents a wider range of choices.
6. *Autonomy.* Because charters schools are free from bureaucratic tangles, they will better serve students and their families.[16]

Accountability
Wells found accountability difficult to evaluate because "the goals and outcomes are often vaguely written and ill-defined; they frequently cover a wide range of desired outcomes, such as the goal of 'enabling pupils to become self-motivated, competent, and lifelong learners'" (20). The goals sections of the chartering documents were often "extremely vague."

Many other researchers comment on how charter operators often write vague goals. This raises a question: Why have so many chartering agencies approved charter schools that did not have appropriate instruments or observations to evaluate the goals? The answer appears to be, at least in part, that most states suffered short staffing with weak granting and oversight agencies. In some cases, such as Arizona, states deliberately created weak accountability systems to give charters as much leeway as possible.

Wells also uncovered what has become another common finding about charters: Schools that lost their charters lost them because they misappropriated or misspent public tax dollars. Charter schools with clean books got their charters renewed even if they had not met the academic goals called for in their contracts.

> *Charter schools with clean books got their charters renewed even if they had not met the academic goals called for in their contracts.*

Efficiency

The UCLA study found that charters need more resources than the publics. They greatly relied on outside, private sources. Some charters had more success at such fund-raising than others. Wells observed that "the claim that charter schools will help prove most public schools are inefficient by doing more with less public funding was not supported by our data. We found no schools doing 'more' with less. We found some poor [charter] schools holding their own with less funding, as they functioned without heat, adequate plumbing, science labs, or any athletic facilities. These schools did not seem efficient, just poor" (61).

Competition

Public schools refused to compete with the charters because public school officials felt the charters had an unfair advantage. They could require parent contracts, could require a certain number of hours of parent involvement, could select students or limit enrollments, had greater hiring autonomy, and had less paperwork. The playing field was not level.

Innovation

Joe Nathan contended that "the charter school movement attempts to promote widespread improvement in public education both by allowing people to create new kinds of schools and by encouraging existing school systems to improve in order to compete effectively with these new schools."[17]

Wells found little in the way of innovation in the schools and even less transfer of innovations. "There are no mechanisms in place for charter schools and regular schools to learn from each other." As a consequence, "all but two of the public school educators we interviewed reported that they had very little information about what was going on in the charter schools and nearly all of the educators we interviewed said they saw little if any direct impact of charter schools on their schools" (54). Indeed, more than a few took the mere existence of the charter schools "as a slap in the face" (55).

Similarly, the charter school operators, who worked long hours, did not see their role as informing other schools about their programs.

The issue of portability—making a successful program in one school work in others—has dogged education since innovations began. Given the conditions just cited, it's hardly surprising that charters' new ideas, where they occurred, didn't percolate through the rest of the district.

Choice

Charter schools did offer more instructional options than the regular publics. The charters also did some choosing. Parent-school contracts as a condition of enrollment have already been mentioned. In addition, few charters provided transportation. Thus, only parents with a vehicle and a flexible schedule could avail themselves of charters.

Autonomy

The UCLA study found mixed results on autonomy. Administrators said that they had the most autonomy in the area of hiring teachers and that this was the area of greatest importance to them. It is important to note here that different states have different approaches to authorizing charter schools and that this greatly affects their autonomy. In California, local school districts authorize virtually all charters (if the district refuses, the charter proponents can appeal, first to the county board and then to the state board). In Michigan, by contrast, public universities authorize most of the charter schools. This gives the charters more autonomy and also requires of them more autonomy.

Recent Data from California

Three reports on California charters appeared in 2003. The largest of these, from the RAND Corporation, added a lot of verbiage but not a lot of information to what we know about California charters in terms of achievement.[18] Indeed, for the nearly three hundred pages of the report, one senses that not only are charters not laboratories of innovation, but they are similar to public schools on virtually every dimension save teacher experience—charter school teachers had less of it.

RAND divided charters into conversions—existing schools that converted their status—and start-ups. The study looked separately at charters that offered instruction only in conventional classrooms and those with at least some portion of instruction outside of classrooms.

Overall, "charter schools have comparable or slightly lower test scores than do conventional public schools" (xxii). However, start-ups and conversions that offered instruction outside of the classroom had lower test scores across the board. For a limited set of school districts that had the necessary technology, RAND was able to track individual students over time. "Overall, the analysis shows that charter school students are keeping pace with comparable students in conventional public schools" (56).

Keeping pace? That is hardly what charter school advocates promised. And it seems particularly disappointing if one asks, "What does it mean to 'keep pace' with public school students in California?" In 2003, California public school fourth graders scored one point above bottom-ranked Louisiana on NAEP reading, and California eighth graders tied Hawaii for last place. "Keeping pace" thus means matching the performance of the lowest-scoring students in the country.

As with the previous evaluations, RAND found little impact of the presence of charters on public schools. "[Our analyses] suggest that conventional public schools have not felt much of a competitive effect from charter schools and have not changed their operational practices significantly" (60).

Contrary to the keeping-pace conclusion of RAND, a study from Margaret Raymond at the Hoover Institution (which in recent years has become something of a retirement home for conservative researchers—Eric Hanushek, Herb Walberg, etc.) claimed to find some advantage for charters, at least at the high school level.[19]

Raymond divided her schools into three categories: traditional, charter, and "local competitor," which were traditional public schools operating in a district that also contained at least one charter school. Given Wells' and RAND's conclusion that charters have little impact on public schools, it is questionable if local competitor is a meaningful category.

California rates its schools with something it calls its Academic Performance Index (and which some people call the Affluent Parents Index because of its high correlation with wealth), made up of test scores. Looking at gains over time, Raymond found no differences among her three categories at the elementary school level. Charters had the smallest gains at the middle school level and the largest gains at the high school level.

Raymond writes, "The striking finding is that their [charter high schools'] average improvement is more than twice that of conventional high schools." Why she did not find it equally striking that gains in charter middle schools were less than half those in traditional and local competitor schools, she does not say.

That she does not say does not matter, says David Rogosa, a statistician at Stanford University.[20] Rogosa says Raymond committed a fundamental statistical blunder. He's right. She did. Raymond started with the average scores of schools, then averaged those scores for each of her categories. That's the problem. Schools differ greatly in size, but Raymond's analysis treats them as if they all contained the same number of students. That means that in her study, small schools got much more weight than they deserved.

Let's take a moment to consider a concrete example to make this point clear. Let's think of New Jersey and Mississippi as if they were schools. In 2002, New Jersey's average verbal SAT score was 498, while Mississippi's was 559. If we simply average these two schools, we get 529. But this "average" makes no sense because New Jersey is a much bigger school than Mississippi and a much higher proportion of its seniors take the SAT. In fact, fifty-nine times as many students sat for the SAT in New Jersey as in Mississippi, 71,163 versus 1,213. If we treat the school as the unit of analysis, the 1,213 kids in Mississippi count just as much as the

71,163 kids in New Jersey. To make the average meaningful, we would have to take into account the differences in size. We might wish to give states of different size equal weight in one house of a bicameral legislature, but in terms of statistics, an average like this makes no sense.

Rogosa's study used the student as the unit of analysis. His conclusion doesn't differ from Raymond's at the elementary level: charters and traditional schools improved about the same amount. But charter high schools gained less and charter middle schools gained much less than traditional public schools. This last finding was especially strong for schools with high proportions of disadvantaged students. At the middle school level, the "gain" in disadvantaged schools was actually a loss, −12.1 points. Rogosa did find a slightly larger gain for disadvantaged elementary charters, but at the middle and high school levels, the direction of change was the reverse of what charter advocates contended would happen—public schools outgained charters.

Michigan

When we turn to Michigan, we see even less of the laboratories-of-innovation effect that charters were supposed to induce than we saw in Arizona or California.

Michigan's charters have received perhaps more attention than those in any other state with evaluations from Western Michigan University,[21,22] Michigan State University,[23,24] Columbia University,[25] the Upjohn Institute for Employment Research,[26] and Public Sector Consultants.[27]

Most of the evaluators have expressed surprise at how similar the charters, known in Michigan as Public School Academies or PSAs, are to the regular public schools. Said Michael Mintrom of Michigan State, "More striking than [the amount of innovation] is the degree of similarity that we find across all schools be they charter or traditional" (iv). Similarly, Western Michigan University's Jerry Horn and Gary Miron commented, "In fact, the charter schools were remarkably similar to the regular public schools, with the notable exception of generally smaller student enrollments, the presence of additional adults in the classroom, governance and the span of contracted services" (1999, 99). Indeed, David Arsen, David Plank, and Gary Sykes from Michigan State even found something of an anti-innovation, not-with-my-kid-you-don't attitude. The parents think that the schools did OK by them and want the same for their children. "Insofar as this is what parents want, PSAs have little to gain and much to lose from experimentation with innovative practices" (57).

In terms of achievement, early investigations found that charters in Michigan's urban areas of Detroit, Flint, and Lansing had slightly better achievement than public schools in those areas. In the rest of the state, the reverse held. The percentage of charter students who passed the Michigan Education Assessment Program (MEAP) tests declined over time. Public school students in the districts that hosted the charter schools increased their pass rate from 48 percent to 68 percent.

Later results have not been kind to charters. They have led to headlines like this one from the *Detroit News* in late 2003: "Substandard Charters Fail 17,000 Pupils." The subheadline of the story was even more devastating: "6 Management Firms Underperform Worst Michigan Urban Districts."[28] Gary Miron and Christopher Nelson put the same results into more dispassionate words:

> We found considerable variation among charters schools, with some clearly out gaining their host districts and others lagging far behind. In the aggregate, however, our findings cast doubt on proponents' claims that Michigan charter schools will leverage gains in student achievement. With the exception of grade four math, MEAP pass rates in the typical charter schools grew less (or fell faster) than those in their host districts.
>
> Finally, we found that, while there are some variations among companies, as a group, charter schools managed by for-profit EMOs gained less (or fell faster) than other charter schools. This casts at least some doubt on privatization advocates' claims that introducing competitive pressures into educational management will lead to improvements in performance.[29]

Horn and Miron were surprised—and put off—by the amount of nepotism they found in the management of Michigan PSAs. However, while the employment of relatives in public service jobs is considered unethical and is often illegal, no such rules constrain the private sector, and most of Michigan's PSAs are run by private firms. Some in the private sector hold that the employment of relatives is a good thing because people will work harder for something that is in the family.

As noted, private firms run most of Michigan's charters. It was not always thus. In 1995, only 16 percent of PSAs were operated by the educational management organizations (EMOs). By 2002, the proportion had increased to 75 percent. Most states do not provide start-up funds, and by operating through an EMO, charters can access private capital. In addition, as noted, the early charter advocates envisioned communities of like-minded people electing to start a charter to realize some educational vision. Without some real-world training and skills in administration, finance, and personnel, this vision will likely not materialize. EMOs, although not models of efficiency, likely did bring some needed managerial, personnel, and fiscal management skills to groups of people not trained in these areas. The EMOs operating most of the PSAs are for-profit companies such as National Heritage Schools and the Leona Group.

However, an analysis of several EMOs by Western Michigan's Gary Miron and Christopher Nelson found them to do worse than charters run by non-EMOs.[30] This is the same conclusion reached by the *Detroit News,* but the *News* conducted its own study and did not publish the methodology.

The PSAs have had some impact on public schools, both positive and negative. In small districts and those with declining populations, the drain from public schools has caused a reduction in support services and school maintenance. This impact is minimized by the fact that most students enter PSAs in kindergarten and don't ever show up on public school rolls.

Some districts have added new services to compete with charters such as before- and after-school programs, all-day kindergartens, foreign languages in elementary grades, increased safety measures, clearer mission statements, and more open and receptive relationships with parents. Overall, though, Horn and Miron couldn't find much: "After nearly five years of operation in Michigan, we conclude that (i) the state's charter schools are producing few and limited innovations; (ii) few schools are implementing comprehensive accountability plans; and (iii) the extensive involvement of EMOs is creating new 'pseudo' school districts in which decisions are made from great distances rather than at the school level" (2000, vii).

Ohio

In Ohio, the profit motive has played a larger role than in the other three states reviewed so far. The atmosphere in which charter schools were established and under which they operate was described in a six-part series by two investigative reporters at the *Akron Beacon Journal*, Dennis Willard and Doug Oplinger.[31] These two reporters did not find education enthusiasts or idealists for the most part. The opening paragraphs in their series read as follows:

> Ohio, already No. 1 in the 90s for putting public dollars into private schools[32] and last in the nation for placing children in safe and sanitary buildings, is on course to earn a new distinction in the next decade.
>
> The state is ready to rival Arizona, California, Florida and Michigan for funneling state and local tax dollars to a new class of schools—charter schools—that are public in some ways and private in others . . .
>
> Less than five months into the second year [of charter school funding]—as charter schools move from concept to reality—serious questions and disturbing problems are starting to arise.
>
> Private, profit-minded companies, known as education management organizations, are making strong inroads into the state. In doing so, these EMOs are concentrating school ownership in the hands of a few and brushing aside the people who were to be given control of their local charter, or community schools—parents, teachers and community members.
>
> ■ The Ohio Board of Education, responsible for oversight, is rubberstamping contracts as fast as it can without thoroughly reviewing the written proposals or hearing from a single charter school representative. One reason: Most board members say they have almost no authority to reject a proposal.
>
> ■ Lawmakers did not fund an oversight office for charter schools until the program's second year and after more than 60 contracts had been approved and 15 schools had opened. The undermanned office is hard-pressed to com-

plete routine checks for fire safety and criminal back-grounds, and is barely monitoring academic progress.

■ Children are bearing the brunt of the charter school prob-lems. The state has allowed charter schools to open with-out textbooks or indoor toilets. Students have attended class in unsafe buildings that lacked sprinklers or fire alarm systems. And local police in Columbus were called 12 times in two months to one charter school to investigate disturbances, including one case of sexual assault.

■ Most charter schools are not models for reform. First-year test scores indicate students in charter schools are doing dramatically worse than public school children, and the new schools are not incubators for innovation as propo-nents promised they would be.

■ Profits are being reaped, but there is no evidence that char-ter schools are reducing education costs or saving Ohio taxpayers money—despite lower pay for teachers and exemptions from 191 state mandates that hike the cost of education in public schools. (1999a, 30)

Charters, called community schools in Ohio, are permitted only in Ohio's eight largest urban areas. No group like Western Michigan's Evaluation Center has formally evaluated Ohio's char-ters. The Ohio legislature established the Legislative Office of Education Oversight (LOEO), but, according to sources in Ohio, if the LOEO brings in a report that the legislature doesn't like, the legislature starts thinking about getting rid of it.

The LOEO has produced five charter school reports, each concentrating on different aspects of the charter experiment. The first-year report found that, although required by law to provide annual reports to parents, most did not and most charter school directors claimed they did not even know they should.[33] The next year, although reporting had gotten better, the LOEO still com-plained that "information critical to the accountability of these schools continues to be missing."[34]

The LOEO in its second-year report noted that charter school teachers had only 4.2 years of experience and received an average salary of only $22,070. The average public school teacher in dis-tricts where charters operated had 14.8 years of experience and was paid an average salary of $43,162, almost double a commu-nity school's average. The low salaries account for the fact that the largest charter school operator in Ohio, White Hat Management, is also one of the few profitable EMOs.

In its third report, the LOEO examined the performance of the fifteen oldest charters (there are now 92 total), which would have been in operation for three years.[35] It found that although neither charter schools nor matched public schools did as well as the state as a whole on the state's fourth- and sixth-grade proficiency tests, the public schools outperformed the charters. None of the charters met the state's passing-level requirement of a 75 percent pass rate. Schools that fail to meet this criterion must improve by 2.5 percentage points per year. Two charters met this requirement in the fourth grade and two different schools met it in the sixth grade. When the LOEO compared actual scores, rather than passing rates, it found that seven of ten possible comparisons were statistically significant and all favored traditional schools.

Despite low performance, more charter school parents gave their schools an A or a B than did traditional school parents, 81 percent versus 68 percent. There might well be some cognitive dissonance in the charter school parents accounting for the difference: if you choose a school for your child, it is likely harder to think ill of it (and therefore admit you made a mistake) than to simply accept the neighborhood school the district assigns your child to attend.

Teachers in traditional schools were slightly more likely to give their schools an A or a B, 66 percent versus 55 percent. Students were the least satisfied. Fifty-five percent of those in charters rated their charter an A or a B, compared with 51 percent of those in traditional schools.

In the fifth and final report from the LOEO, issued October 28, 2003, one senses a palpable frustration from the report's authors that they have *still* been unable to get the information they need—and which the state requires—in order to completely evaluate community schools.[36] One senses that if political diplomacy did not dictate silence, the LOEO would like to accuse some charters of *deliberately* withholding needed information and data. There is a hope that the reporting requirements for No Child Left Behind might—finally!—force the charter schools to comply.

The final report generally affirms the performance advantage of traditional schools noted in the third report. On only the writing test did the charters match the publics. When the LOEO compared charters and traditionals as groups, fourteen of twenty comparisons were statistically significant and thirteen of those favored traditionals.

When each charter was compared with the individual traditional school with which it had been matched, almost two-thirds of the comparisons (270 of 415) were not statistically significant. Of the 145 comparisons that did reach significance, 103 favored traditional schools and 42 favored charters.

The LOEO was not, however, able to make comparisons for all schools it wanted to.

> When community schools fail to report the required data, it impedes the ability of LOEO and the General Assembly to evaluate the performance of the movement. Instead of appraising their academic achievement with data from 50 community schools, only 32 schools were included in the comparison of proficiency test scores with similar traditional schools. Only 17 schools provided the necessary proficiency test data for all their years of operation for comparison with the performance goals specified in their contracts. (12)

The report continued:

> Taking all the comparisons together, the most that can be said about the academic performance of community schools is that, as a group, they are doing no better than low-performing traditional public schools with similar demographic characteristics. While most community schools are not meeting state academic standards, many are not reporting data that allow them to be compared to their contracts. Those that do report data are generally not meeting the academic performance goals specified in their contracts. (26)

It is not that the community schools do not know that they have to report certain data. They do. They know that, in the words of the report,

> In Ohio, there are three primary components of accountability for community schools: 1) academic achievement, 2) financial viability, and 3) parent choice and satisfaction. Three reporting mechanisms are used to describe how community schools are performing on these components of accountability: community school annual reports, Local Report Cards issue by the Ohio

Department of Education, and financial audits reported by the Auditor of the states. Only one of these mechanisms is effective for reporting on accountability: the Auditor of State reports. Annual reports are often submitted late and lack required information. Local Report Cards are often based on incomplete and inaccurate data. (57–58)

The LOEO appears to sense that this report might be its last opportunity to improve the community school situation. It wraps up its report with some strong recommendations and argues that if the Ohio Department of Education and the charter school sponsors do not comply, the legislature should terminate funding:

LOEO recommends that the General Assembly continue to support the community school initiative only if it requires the Ohio Department of Education and community school sponsors to do the following:

The Ohio Department of Education:
Determine why community schools are submitting such poor EMIS data (Education Management Information System), and design technical assistance for these schools based on these findings.

More closely monitor the accuracy of EMIS data submitted by community schools, and enforce financial penalties for schools that provide inaccurate data.

Report the number of students who have withdrawn from community schools on their Local Report Cards.

As a condition of approving a sponsor, require sponsors to ensure that contract goals are clear and measurable.

Community School Sponsors:
Penalize community schools for late, incomplete, or inaccurate data. Such penalties could include placing a school on probation or not renewing its contract.

Before contracts are approved, insist that the student achievement and attendance goals are clear, that the manner in which they will be measured has been specified, and that the standard for success has been identified.

Base the contract renewal process on the specific goals in each school's contract, not on a general rubric. (60–61; emphasis in original)

It will be interesting to see if the Ohio legislature, which has not shown any backbone concerning community schools or vouchers to date, will act on the LOEO's recommendations. This is the same lawmaking body that, shortly after a study found that Cleveland public school students had gained more than voucher-using students, expanded the voucher program by $10.5 million.

Washington, D.C.

Charter schools in Washington, D.C., have received scrutiny from both educational researchers and journalists. Jeffrey Henig of George Washington University (now at Columbia) and colleagues Thomas Holyoke, Natalie Lacireno-Paquet, and Michelle Moser, found that charter schools in the District of Columbia had fewer special education students. In spite of this, tests showed large differences in favor of the public schools.[37] Even when Henig grouped schools into categories based on percent of students from low-income homes, percent with language needs, and percent in special education, public school students substantially outperformed those in the charters.

This categorization is important because it is often claimed that charter schools do worse because they deal with harder-to-educate kids. Clearly the Henig study shows that, for D.C. at least, when schools are matched, the publics still do better. (One can only imagine the outrage that would show up on op-ed pages if public schools tried to use the "harder-to-educate kids" excuse. Public school educators have on occasion pointed out that they take anyone in the attendance zone, and they usually hear something to the effect of "Poverty is no excuse.")

A team of researchers at George Washington University tested the hypothesis that charters "cream" students, that they take the academically more able.[38] They found no evidence of this. They found, though, a process they labeled "cropping." Charters that had a market orientation cropped out certain categories of hard-to-educate—more expensive—children. They had lower percentages of special education students and students from low-income families.

When Justin Blum and Jay Mathews of the *Washington Post* took a look at the District's charters, they came away with test statistics that are more recent than those in the Henig study but which also affirm the higher performance of public schools.[39]

They also cast doubt on the argument that parents choose charters for good reasons: Most parents interviewed about their decision to enroll their children in charter schools said they did not bother to look at test scores or other data. Some were swayed by tours, some by comments from friends, or by a creative curriculum that seemed to match their child's needs. "Others turned to charters mostly because of the regular school system's poor reputation . . . Phonshanta Franklin said friends told her to avoid the regular schools after she moved from Maryland to Southeast Washington. She picked her four children's charter schools based largely on which ones had space and were closest to her home" (Blum and Mathews 2003).

The Blum and Mathews series also deflated the argument that charters will cause the public schools to improve. Between 1996 and 2002–2003, the number of students in charter schools grew from zero to 11,603, while D.C.'s enrollment slumped from 78,648 to 66,852, but D.C. did not react to the losses. "Contrary to the predictions of many charter school advocates, the vigorous competition from charters has not forced improvements in the regular public schools . . . The consensus among school officials, parents and education analysts is that the charters' success in attracting students has not prompted much change at the traditional schools," according to Blum and Mathews. They quote Robert Maranto of Villanova: "People like me who said, 'Competition will raise all boats,' were wrong."

Blum and Mathews note that while public school enrollment declined in the 1996–2002 period, few individual D.C. public schools felt a large loss of pupils. In addition, the per-pupil spending over the 1996–2002 period increased. Blum and Mathews cite these facts as reasons that the loss of enrollment was cushioned. It was also true that a new superintendent arrived with his own school improvement program that was independent of anything happening in charters.

It seems to me, though, that Blum and Mathews overlooked one obvious explanation for the publics not reacting to the charters: on average, the public schools have higher test scores. What are they to learn from the charters other than that they need to make the public more aware of their own higher performance?

In sum, charters have not delivered results in keeping with the Nathan Criterion. In the early years, people were wont to say, "It's too soon to tell." But charters have been around for twelve years, and while no doubt some excellent charter schools exist, so do many excellent public schools. Charters have not received the criticism they would have, in part because, overall, public school enrollments have soared since 1985 and charters' potential financial impact on school revenues has been thereby diminished. But in many places charters are draining off students and dollars. The profit from a student who attends an Edison school in Michigan, California, Ohio, or Arizona goes to Edison headquarters in New York, not into the community.

Charter schools were born of perceived failures in public schools. So, if charters are doing worse than the publics, where is the outrage about them?

Charter schools were born of perceived failures in public schools. So, if charters are doing worse than the publics, where is the outrage about them?

Notes

1. American Federation of Teachers (AFT). 2003. *Do Charter Schools Measure Up? The Charter School Experiment After Ten Years*. Washington, DC: AFT.

2. Nathan, Joe. 1996. *Charter Schools: Bringing Hope and Opportunity to American Education*. Berkeley, CA: Jossey-Bass, xxx.

3. Hill, Paul, Robin Lake, Mary Beth Celio, Christine Campbell, Paul Hardman, and Katrina Bulkley. 2001. *A Study of Charter School Accountability*. Seattle: Center on Reinventing Public Education, University of Washington, vii.

4. Finn, Chester E., Louann Bierlein, and Bruno V. Manno. 1996. *Charter Schools in Action: A First Look*. Washington, DC: Hudson Institute.

5. Manno, Bruno V. 1999. *Accountability: The Key to Charter School Reform*. Washington, DC: Center for Education Reform.

6. Henig, Jeffrey R. 1994. *Rethinking School Choice: Limits of the Market Metaphor*. Princeton, NJ: Princeton University Press.

7. Bulkley, Katrina. 2001. "The Accountability Bind." *Education Policy Analysis Archives*. *http://epaa.asu.edu/epaa/v9n37.html*.

8. Brennan, Deborah. 2000. "A Lesson in Hard Knocks as Charter School Closes." *Los Angeles Times,* 25 June, A28.

9. Toch, Thomas. 1998. "The New Education Bazaar." *U.S. News and World Report,* 27 April, 24.

10. Ibid.

11. Cobb, Casey, and Gene V. Glass. 1998. "Ethnic Segregation in Arizona Charter Schools." *Education Policy Analysis Archives*. *http://epaa.asu.edu/epaa/v7n1*.

12. Hunter, Bruce, Associate Executive Director, American Association of School Administrators (AASD). 2004. Personal communication.

13. Frankenburg, Erica, and Chungmei Lee. 2003. *Charter Schools and Race: A Lost Opportunity for Integrated Education*. Cambridge, MA: Civil Rights Project, Harvard University.

14. Solmon, Lewis, Kern Paark, and David Garcia. 2001. *Does Charter School Attendance Improve Test Scores?* Phoenix: Goldwater Institute, 4.

15. Nelson, Christopher, and David Hollenbeck. 2001. *"Does Charter School Attendance Improve Test Scores?" Comments and Reactions on the Arizona Achievement Study*. Kalamazoo, MI: W. E. Upjohn Institute for Employment Research.

16. Wells, Amy Stuart. 1998. *Beyond the Rhetoric of Charter School Reform*. Los Angeles: University of California at Los Angeles.

17. Nathan, Joe. 1996. *Charter Schools: Bringing Hope and Opportunity to American Education*. Berkeley, CA: Jossey-Bass, 13.

18. Zimmer, Ron, Richard Buddin, Derrick Chau, Brian Gill, Cassandra Guarino, Laura Hamilton, Cathy Krop, Dan McCaffrey, Melinda Sandler, and Dominic Bewer. 2003. *Charter School Operations and Performance: Evidence from California*. Santa Monica, CA: RAND.

19. Raymond, Margaret. 2003. *The Performance of California Charter Schools*. Stanford, CA: Hoover Institution.

20. Rogosa, David. 2003. *Student Progress in California Charter Schools*. Available at *www.cde.ca.gov/psaa/apiresearch.htm*; look under the category "Other reports of interest."

21. Horn, Jerry, and Gary Miron. 1999. *Evaluation of the Michigan*

Charter School Initiative. Kalamazoo, MI: Evaluation Center, Western Michigan University.

22. Horn, Jerry, and Gary Miron. 2000. *An Evaluation of the Michigan Charter School Initiative: Performance, Accountability, and Impact.* Kalamazoo, MI: Evaluation Center, Western Michigan University.

23. Arsen, David, David Plank, and Gary Sykes. 1999. *School Choice Policies in Michigan: The Rules Matter.* East Lansing, MI: Michigan State University.

24. Mintrom, Michael. 1998. *Michigan's Charter School Movement.* East Lansing, MI: Michigan State University.

25. Bettinger, Eric. 1998. *The Effect of Charter Schools on Charter Students and Public Schools.* Occasional Paper #4. New York: National Center for the Study of Privatization in Education, Columbia University.

26. Eberts, Randall W., and Kevin M. Hollenbeck. 2001. *An Examination of Student Achievement in Michigan Charter Schools.* Kalamazoo, MI: W. E. Upjohn Institute for Employment Research.

27. Khouri, Nick, Robert Kleine, Richard White, and Laura Cummings. 1999. *Michigan's Charter School Initiative: From Theory to Practice.* Lansing, MI: Public Sector Consultants.

28. Heath, Brad. 2003. "Substandard Charters Fail 17,000 Pupils: 6 Management Firms Underperform Worst Michigan Urban Districts." *The Detroit News,* 26 October, A1.

29. Miron, Gary, and Christopher Nelson. 2003. *What Do We Know About Achievement in Charter Schools and Why We Know So Little.* Kalamazoo, MI: Evaluation Center, Western Michigan University.

30. Miron, Gary, and Christopher Nelson. 2002. *What's Public About Charter Schools?* Thousand Oaks, CA: Corwin Press.

31. Willard, Dennis J., and Doug Oplinger. 1999a. "Charter Experiment Goes Awry: Schools Fail to Deliver," "Voucher Plan Leaves Long List of Broken Promises," "School Battle Eludes Voters, Takes Its Cues from Coalitions." *Akron Beacon Journal,* 12 December, 14 December, and 15 December, A1; Oplinger, Doug, and Dennis J. Willard. 1999b. "In Education, Money Talks," "Voucher Plan Falls Far Short of Goals," "Campaign Organizer Pushes Hard for Changes." *Akron Beacon Journal,* 13 December, 14 December, and 15 December, A1.

32. This is true, but not because of the onset of charters, vouchers, or other forms or privatization. Ohio has a long history of state support

for private schools, support that is substantially greater than in any other state.

33. Legislative Office of Education Oversight (LOEO). 2000. *Community Schools in Ohio: First-Year Implementation Report.* Columbus, OH: LOEO.

34. Legislative Office of Education Oversight (LOEO). 2001. *Community Schools in Ohio, Second-Year Implementation Report, Volume 1: Policy Issues.* Columbus, OH: LOEO.

35. Legislative Office of Education Oversight (LOEO). 2002. *Community Schools in Ohio, Third-Year Implementation Report.* Columbus, OH: LOEO.

36. Legislative Office of Education Oversight (LOEO). 2003. *Community Schools in Ohio: Final Report on Student Achievement, Parent Satisfaction, and Accountability.* Columbus, OH: LOEO.

37. Henig, Jeffrey R., Thomas T. Holyoke, Natalie Lacireno-Paquet, and Michele Moser. 2001. *Growing Pains: An Evaluation of Charter Schools in the District of Columbia, 1999–2000.* Washington, DC: George Washington University.

38. Lacireno-Paquet, Natalie, Thomas Holyoke, Michele Moser, and Jeffrey R. Henig. 2002. "Creaming vs. Cropping: Charter School Enrollment Practices in Response to Market Incentives." *Educational Evaluation and Policy Analysis* (summer): 145–58.

39. Blum, Justin, and Jay Mathews. 2003. "Quality Uneven, Despite Popularity." *Washington Post,* 19 June, A1; Blum, Justin. 2003. "Staying the Course Despite Competition." *Washington Post,* 20 June, A1.

9 Vouchers
A Good Way to Destroy Public Schools

What do I say when people say, "We should just give families vouchers and let the money follow the child. Let the parents choose what schools to send their kids to. Good schools would flourish, bad schools would go out of business, and the whole system would improve"?

You can say, "Such a system would fundamentally alter our society, killing our communal, democratic form and changing it into one that treats all human interactions the same as buying a Big Mac—a commercial transaction. It would kill public debate on what we ought to teach in schools. And, so far, vouchers haven't improved the education of those who have used them or those in schools that are supposedly getting better by competing with voucher schools."

The concept of vouchers is not new and not limited to schools. Food stamps, Medicaid, and some subsidized housing are all examples of vouchers. The English philosopher John Stuart Mill is usually credited with formulating the modern concept of vouchers. In his 1838 essay "On Liberty," Mill expressed outrage that the state did not force parents to educate their children, a function he considered among parents' "most sacred duties."[1] Mill put his basic position thusly:

> If the government were to make up its mind to *require* for every child a good education, it might save itself the trouble of *providing* one. It might leave to parents to obtain the education where and how they pleased, and content itself with helping to pay the school fees of the poor classes of children, and defraying the entire school expenses of those who have no one else to pay for them. (117, emphasis in original)

The state needed educated citizens, Mill declared, but the state, whether a dictatorship or a democracy or some other form of government, would use schooling only to mold children into its desired shape, not to educate them.

In the late 1950s, economist Milton Friedman updated Mill's idea and then elaborated it in his 1962 book, *Freedom and Capitalism*. One person who was convinced by Friedman's book was Ronald Reagan, who advocated vouchers as part of his education agenda when he became president in 1980.

Arguments for vouchers are very much the same as for charter schools, with one addition: advocates claim vouchers will empower people of no means to obtain a good education for their children. The poor cannot afford private school tuition, nor can they afford to move to the suburbs, where, even the harshest public school critics concede, the schools are pretty good. If the money follows the children to whatever schools they attend, the poor can escape their dysfunctional neighborhood schools. Of course, it might start a taxpayer revolt if parents whose children attended those good schools already were not permitted to keep them there. This is a distinct possibility under the No Child Left Behind Act of 2001. Any school that NLCB declares "needs improvement" must offer all children in that school the option of transferring to one with higher test scores.

Resultant crowding in the receiving school is no excuse for denying the transfers access. The receiving school must "build capacity." This could lead to dysfunctionally large classes or, less likely, to the receiving school's trying to maintain smaller classes by denying access to some of those who live in the neighborhood.

As of early 2004, parents had made no mad rush to get their children out of "failing" schools. Many question the designation of "failing school," particularly as a school receives that label if any one subgroup in the school fails to make Adequate Yearly Progress or even if the school cannot manage to test 95 percent of the group. In addition, people cling to their neighborhood schools more than free-market advocates think. "It's easier to move a cemetery than to close a school," goes an old saw.

> As of early 2004, parents had made no mad rush to get their children out of "failing" schools.

In the few instances where parents in one district have

applied to have their children attend schools in other districts, the would-be receiving districts have rejected the applications. Administrative problems have been cited, but accusations of racism have been uttered—the students in the sending district were black, those in the receiving district mostly white.[2]

Studies have found little evidence that vouchers accomplish what their advocates claim. In addition, none of the small experiments currently in progress will provide good evidence for whether or not vouchers would work on a large scale, even if they did lead to improvements on a small scale. Terry Moe of the Hoover Institution, himself an ardent voucher advocate, explained well why the experiments to date have little relevance to other experiments or to the effect of voucher use on a large scale:

> Ideology aside, perhaps the most vexing problem [of voucher research] is that few researchers who carry out studies of school choice are sensitive to issues of institutional design or context. They proceed as though their case studies reveal something generic about choice or markets when, in fact—as the Milwaukee case graphically testifies—much of what they observe is due to the specific rules, restrictions, and control mechanisms that shape how choice and markets happen to operate. As any economist would be quick to point out, the effects of choice and markets vary, sometimes enormously, depending on the institutional context. The empirical literature on school choice does little to shed light on these contingencies and, indeed, by portraying choice and markets as generic reforms with generic effects, often breeds more confusion than understanding. (20)[3]

One voucher proponent, Paul Peterson of Harvard, listed nine constraints on the Milwaukee program and likened them to Dante's nine circles of Hell. Peterson thought that because, in his analyses (rejected by others), the voucher kids did better, it meant that choice worked in spite of the constraints. If vouchers could overcome such hardships, Peterson contended in a debate at the Cato Institute, they will work anywhere. His counter, Jeffrey Henig, then of George Washington University, now at Columbia, presented the Moe argument—so many aspects of the Milwaukee program applied only to Milwaukee, it was impossible to generalize the results.

Moe has said that it is not the case that choice is choice is choice. In some instances, the "specific rules, restrictions and control mechanisms" that Moe mentions in general caused advocates and researchers to advocate different things. For instance, in the Milwaukee voucher program, if a school had more applicants than spaces, it had to admit the applicants at random. From a researcher's perspective, this is ideal. Random assignment assures that there will be no systematic source of bias that could cause differences between those admitted and those rejected, such as income differences or differences in parental education level. An advocate would prefer that a school be able to choose those whom it admits. It could then more carefully match the school's programs to the applicants' needs. Advocates argue that a school-student match is more likely to lead to success.

Some larger-scale voucher programs might come into existence as a result of a Supreme Court decision. In June 2003, the Supreme Court declared that the Cleveland voucher program was not unconstitutional even though virtually all children attended religious schools. This has emboldened some state legislators to consider statewide programs. Most states, though, have even stricter constraints in their constitutions than the federal constitution on sending public money to private, especially religious, schools. These clauses would have to be either rewritten or dropped through referenda or challenged in court.

Soon after the Supreme Court's Cleveland ruling, the Colorado legislature did pass voucher legislation, providing for use of vouchers worth $4,500 a year in Colorado's eleven largest districts. The law limited the 2004–2005 vouchers to 1 percent of a district's enrollment and capped the figure at 6 percent in 2008. In December 2003, Denver District Court Judge Joseph E. Meyer III ruled the law unconstitutional.[4] Advocates appealed, but on June 28, 2004, the Colorado Supreme Court upheld Judge Meyer's decision.[5]

The best known public voucher programs are those in Milwaukee and Cleveland, to which we now turn.

Milwaukee

In Milwaukee, legislation passed in 1990 permitted up to 1 percent of the students to attend private schools using public funds.

The cap has since been raised to 15 percent. In 2003–2004, some thirteen thousand children used vouchers at a cost of $80 million. Up to 2001–2002, state aid to Milwaukee was cut to cover 50 percent of these costs and aid to the other 425 Wisconsin districts was reduced to cover the other half. Beginning in 2001–2002, Milwaukee bore all of the loss and could only recoup by raising property taxes.

In a suit, a lower court ruled the program unconstitutional. The Wisconsin Supreme Court, though, decided that the program passed constitutional muster. Despite the fact that both sides in the suit urged the U.S. Supreme Court to hear the case, it declined to.

Something of a scandal erupted when it was learned that wealthy voucher advocates across the nation had contributed hundreds of thousands of dollars to the election campaign of a voucher-advocating judge who was running for a seat on the state supreme court. Contributors included Patrick Rooney of Golden Rule Insurance in Indiana ($34,500) and John Walton of Wal-Mart ($25,000). The judge won. State Superintendent John T. Benson commented, "It is obvious that people who made contributions to this justice's campaign had one thing in mind, and that was to elect someone who would be an advocate for the voucher system."[6]

The Wisconsin Department of Public Instruction commissioned John Witte and colleagues at the University of Wisconsin to evaluate the program's effectiveness for each of the first five years. Their final report concluded that voucher students did not differ from a matched sample of public school students.[7] Researchers at Harvard, however, reanalyzed the data and concluded that voucher students outscored public school students.[8]

How the Harvard researchers handled their results is instructive. Normally, researchers conduct a study, write up a draft, and send it to colleagues for review. They then present to the relevant professional organization(s). After considering reviews of colleagues and reactions from the presentation, they then send it to a journal, preferably one that sends the manuscript out for blind review by peers in the field. If the peers concur that the research has merit, the journal publishes it and it enters the realm of public discourse.

That is not how Greene and Peterson delivered their study. They released it first to the media, two weeks before they presented it to any professional organization. On the day of the release, the two senior authors had an op-ed in the *Wall Street Journal* slamming Witte and colleagues, titled "Choice Data Rescued from Bad Science"[9] (while the *Wall Street Journal* offers fairly balanced and extensive reporting on education, its editorial page lives up to the moniker given it by a *Slate* writer: a viper's nest of right-wing vitriol). That day happened to be the day that Robert Dole, the Republican candidate for president, addressed the Republican national convention and called for vouchers. Within hours, former Secretaries of Education Lamar Alexander and William J. Bennett appeared on television talk shows touting the study. "How *can* we deny these children," said Alexander, "now that we *know* vouchers work?" Noted pedagogue Rush Limbaugh used his program to send the good news over the air.

Advocacy-Laced "Research": A Troubling Trend

The departure of Greene and Peterson from the usual techniques of assuring objectivity in research is part of a troubling trend: the infusion of ideology into science. Dubious research has been appearing rather often from such institutions as the Heritage Foundation, the Manhattan Institute, the Hoover Institution, and even some university-based researchers.

In the Bush administration, the penetration has accelerated. A March 2004 article in *Education Week* about this problem as part of the Bush administration agenda appeared over this headline: "In Bush Administration, Policies Drive Science, Scholars' Group Claims."[10]

The "scholars' group" consisted of sixty scientists, including a dozen Nobel Laureates, and was released by the Union of Concerned Scientists. According to one of them, David M. Michaels, a professor of environmental and occupational health at George Washington University, "In previous administrations, the policymakers asked scientists to provide the best scientific evidence, and then it was up to the policymakers to make their own decisions. What's going on now is that the science is being misrepresented and repressed so that it is made to look like it supports the policymakers' decisions, and that's a big difference."[11]

"Science is very much under attack with the Bush administration," said Representative Henry A. Waxman (D-California). "If the science doesn't fit what the White House wants it to be, it distorts the science to fit into what its preconceived notions are about what it wants to do."[12] Waxman's office issued a report detailing political interference in twenty areas.[13] Examples include deleting information from websites, stacking advisory committees with candidates with uncertain qualifications and questionable industry ties, and suppressing information and projects inconvenient to White House policy goals, such as those dealing with global warming. Waxman observed that a "hit list" of 120 researchers was put together by the Traditional Values Coalition. To Keith R. Yamamoto, executive dean at the medical school of the University of San Francisco, the message was clear: "Look out: Big Brother is watching."[14]

Research on women's issues seems to have been singled out for attack according to *Missing: Information About Women's Lives*.[15] A report from CDC on condom effectiveness was changed to cast doubt on their effectiveness. A National Cancer Institute report was changed to make it appear that abortion was linked to breast cancer when, in fact, the report said there was no such link. A Health and Human Services report was altered to make abstinence-only programs appear more effective.

In education, the most egregious examples—that we know about—were the distortions of the technical report of the National Reading Panel that appeared in the summary report of that panel. A number of "findings" in the summary report are not supported by the technical report. [16, 17, 18]

This is rather chilling and very much evokes George Orwell's *1984,* whose principal if invisible character, Big Brother, was evoked by Dean Yamamoto above. Orwell's novel invented the concept of "the memory hole." When documents went down the memory hole, their contents, or the people identified in them, not only ceased to exist but ceased to have ever existed. With reports stored in cyberspace, information *can* disappear and leave no record of ever having existed.

Other researchers also reanalyzed the Milwaukee data. Perhaps the most disinterested analysis was conducted by Cecilia

Rouse, an economist at Princeton. She found an effect for mathematics favoring voucher students, but no effect for reading. She also concluded later that the effect was at least as likely due to the small classes in the voucher schools as to any "voucher" effect.[19] Rouse analyzed the data using public schools that had class sizes as small as those in the voucher schools. The effect favoring voucher schools completely disappeared. (A nonresearcher might, at this point, wonder why different researchers would come to different conclusions with the "same" data. The answer lies in the assumptions they make about aspects of the data—how to handle missing data, for instance, or the importance or nonimportance of personal background information in a random-assignment experiment. The field typically accepts the studies whose analysts have best justified their assumptions.)

Researcher Howard Nelson, examining an earlier Rouse analysis, observed that not only did Rouse not agree with Greene and Peterson, but her analysis provided a stinging rebuke to how Greene and Peterson conducted their analyses. He described thirteen ways in which Rouse's methods differed from Greene and Peterson's all of them favoring Rouse in terms of scientific rigor.[20]

I present all of this discussion to illustrate how hard it is to get objective reports about the impact of vouchers. For me, the entire flap over the Milwaukee program is much ado about very little, maybe nothing. I draw this conclusion because the data are so flawed. Among the problems:

- Researchers could collect data only on unsuccessful voucher applicants who entered Milwaukee Public Schools, not on those who went to private schools anyway or to other districts. These were fewer than half of those rejected. This makes for a crucial flaw in Greene and Peterson's analyses. They contended that because students were admitted to voucher schools by lottery, those who were rejected form a natural control group that is comparable with those admitted. But, fewer than half of those rejected turned up in MPS schools and this group might very well differ from those who were rejected and went elsewhere.

- Parents responded to surveys at low rates and at different rates—only 37 percent of the voucher families and 22 percent of the MPS families. Some analyses used this data to control for family background characteristics.

■ The low survey response rate meant that test scores *and* survey data were available for only 28 percent of the voucher students and 21 percent of the MPS students.

■ Random selection into voucher schools, much emphasized by Greene and Peterson, occurred only at schools that were oversubscribed. One of the two schools enrolling most of the African American students admitted everyone who applied, while the other had a waiting list.

■ Siblings of already admitted students could skip the lottery.

■ Voucher applicants with "disabilities" could be rejected with no oversight or supervision of the process. Given that most private schools have minimal programs and expertise in special education, one wonders what conditions they might have seen as "disabilities" and whether specialists in public schools would have agreed with the diagnoses.

I present this extended discussion of methodological problems as a concrete example of the kinds of constraints Moe was talking about in general. What initially looks like a simple theoretical question subject to easy empirical tests—do voucher kids outperform public school kids?—turns out in reality to be immensely complex.

What initially looks like a simple theoretical question subject to easy empirical tests—do voucher kids outperform public school kids?—turns out in reality to be immensely complex.

One might think that given the debate, the various interpretations, and the absence of clarity, the state of Wisconsin might expend more money and effort to obtain evaluations that would clarify things. No. Voucher advocates pushed the legislature to kill all funds for evaluation. There has not been any money—or data—forthcoming since 1995. Those who sought to conduct evaluations using other funds have also been stymied because the Archdiocese of Milwaukee, whose schools contain most voucher students, has refused to make the test scores of voucher students available to researchers. That suggests the scores are not very good.

Even in the absence of formal research, some fascinating iso-lated facts are known. At some private schools, more than 90 per-cent of the students are voucher students. At one Catholic school, two-thirds of the teachers quit rather than cope with the voucher students. Private school enrollment since the onset of the voucher program has declined.[21] Given that there are 13,000 voucher stu-dents, this means that the private schools have been losing stu-dents. This is not, according to voucher advocates and market theorists, how it is supposed to work.

There is talk of reinstating money for further evaluation. As of mid 2004, it was still just talk.

It is worth a small digression to note that free-market advo-cates argue that for the market to work properly, consumers must have access to good information about the product's quality. This is not happening in Milwaukee. Emily Van Dunk and Anneliese Dickman of Milwaukee's Public Policy Forum write, "Ironically, at a time when great emphasis is being placed on accountability and achievement, there is an accountability void in Wisconsin when it comes to private voucher schools . . . We have found that, overall parental knowledge of specific schools tends to be low, and that parents face considerable barriers in their efforts to obtain infor-mation about schools. Thus, parents are unable, by themselves, to hold schools fully accountable."[22]

Cleveland

In April 1995, the Ohio legislature approved the use of public funds for private school vouchers. The vouchers could be used by students in grades K–3 and were worth up to $2,250. Unlike the Milwaukee program, Cleveland permitted up to 25 percent of the vouchers to go to students already enrolled in private schools. Two private schools that accepted vouchers were those run by David Brennan, an Ohio entrepreneur, former head of the Ohio Republican Party, and chairman of former Governor George Voinovich's Commission on Education Choice. Ohio's charter law forbids private schools from converting to charter school status. This led Brennan to establish a nonprofit firm to operate charter schools. He then shut down his two private schools. Brennan claimed he had no direct governing authority in the nonprofit firm, and that firm proceeded to reopen the two schools as charters. The faculty and the administration remained the same as they had been when the schools were private.

Brennan likely orchestrated this conversion because vouchers brought him only $2,250 per student, but Ohio charter schools at the time (1999) received $4,500 per child.[23]

Harvard's Peterson and Greene, along with William Powell of Stanford, were hired to evaluate the Cleveland program by the right-wing, voucher-advocating John M. Olin Foundation. They claimed to find that the voucher students had gained 5.5 percentile ranks in reading and 15 ranks in math. There was no control group. And, as it turned out, they had evaluated only two of the fifty-five participating schools—the two owned by David Brennan.[24]

The American Federation of Teachers criticized the Peterson study on the grounds that all data came from a fall-to-spring testing. Fall-to-spring testing used to be quite popular in evaluating Title I programs but has been largely abandoned because it overestimates gains. At the most cynical level, people can act in ways that depress scores in the fall and elevate them in the spring. More generally, poor students exhibit a phenomenon that middle-class and affluent students do not: summer loss. They do not sustain the gains over the summer.[25, 26, 27]

A more comprehensive evaluation might have been difficult and/or inconclusive. The largest subgroup of voucher users, 834, or 42 percent, had never been in school before. They used the vouchers to attend kindergarten. The previous year, Cleveland Public Schools had eliminated all-day kindergarten, leaving private schools as the only place harried parents could find it. Another 496 (25 percent) were already in private schools. Only 663 (33 percent) of those who used vouchers in 1996–1997 actually left the public schools to attend private ones.

Controversy attended the Cleveland program. An external audit by the accounting firm of Deloitte and Touche uncovered many questionable payouts. Some of the students were not eligible for vouchers—they didn't live in the right place or didn't attend the right grades or their parents made too much money— more than $50,000 per year for thirty families. One-third of the students did not have the same last name as the adults filing the application, but the program staff had made no attempt to verify guardianship.[28]

The accounting firm could not establish that "the Department of Administrative Services had been involved in the procurement process or that the services for which the Program was billed were actually provided." The program was billed $379,433 for such services. Most questionable was the $1,882,454 that the program spent on transportation. It would have cost $3.33 a day to bus pupils to their schools, but the program spent $15 to $18 per child per day on taxis. In all, Deloitte and Touche found 36 percent of the expenditures to be highly questionable.

Kim Metcalf and colleagues at the Indiana Center for Evaluation, part of Indiana University, evaluated the Cleveland program and in 2003 published a summary of four years' worth of data that they had collected from 1998 through 2001.[29, 30]

One question evaluators always want and need to answer is Who uses vouchers? In Cleveland, white students were overrepresented in comparison to their proportion in the public schools, as were Hispanics and students giving their ethnicity as "multiracial." African Americans were underrepresented.

Students who use vouchers and students who don't tend to be very similar, demographically, at the beginning of the school year. Both groups mostly come from the public schools. However, not all students who are invited to use a voucher do so and these vouchers then go to other students. These students tend to be white, to come from families with higher incomes, and to have attended private schools before receiving the voucher.

What everyone wants to know about a voucher program, of course, is Did it work? Did it raise the achievement of the students who use vouchers? The Center for Evaluation will continue to collect data for a number of years but thus far "the most recent results do not reveal any significant impacts of participation in the Cleveland voucher program on student achievement," according to Metcalf's 1998–2002 report (7).

At the program's inception in 1998, all students in the study were in first grade. In the fall of 1998, public school students who did not apply, public school students who did not receive vouchers, and public school students who received vouchers but did not use them had lower test scores than students who used the vouchers. By spring 1999, these differences had disappeared. Nor have they reappeared, and the students have now finished the fourth grade, according to Metcalf's reports. Writes Metcalf, "student academic achievement . . . presents no clear or consistent pattern that can be attributable to program participation" (1998–2002 report, 10).

Despite the lack of evidence that the Cleveland voucher program works, the Ohio legislature, literally in the dark of night, appropriated $10.5 million in new state aid, an increase of 44 percent. According to media, the money is intended mostly to cut the operating losses of the area's Catholic schools.[31] In 2002–2003, 96 percent of the children using vouchers in Cleveland attended church-affiliated schools, 70 percent attended Catholic schools.

> *Despite the lack of evidence that the Cleveland voucher program works, the Ohio legislature, literally in the dark of night, appropriated $10.5 million in new state aid, an increase of 44 percent.*

Cleveland and Milwaukee are the only two sites of experimental programs with taxpayer-financed vouchers. Several others venues have explored the use of private vouchers. I'll now examine those.

New York City

The most contentious data concerning vouchers have come from New York City. There, William Howell, Patrick Wolf, Paul Peterson, and David Campbell claimed to find a significant voucher effect for African Americans.[32] Mathematica Policy Research joined Peterson and Howell, with David Myers acting as Mathematica's principal investigator. Myers almost immediately disavowed Peterson's characterization of the results.[33]

The New York program used privately funded vouchers. Students were assigned to receive a voucher or not by lottery, a procedure that removes any possible systematic bias (bias by chance is still possible, but not likely). Voucher students and voucher-seeking-but-unsuccessful students were compared in reading and mathematics in grades 3 through 6. Most comparisons did not reach any level of statistical significance. When examined by ethnicity, African American students in the sixth grade showed large test score gains. It was large enough, in fact, to make the outcome for African Americans taken as a whole across the four grades significant.

Some questioned the lumping of the four grades. Myers said, "Because the gains are so concentrated in this single group (sixth grade), one needs to be very cautious."

"An average is an average," said Peterson.[34] In fact, in their book *The Education Gap: Vouchers and Urban Schools,* Peterson and Howell went on to recommend that "states offer vouchers to all families regardless of income, who live within a central city district" (89). In this book Peterson also speculated that maybe black public schools were worse than white or Latino schools, or, because almost all black students using vouchers were in Catholic schools, maybe "a missionary commitment is required to create a positive educational environment" for blacks.[35]

As with Milwaukee, other researchers looked at the data and found other results. In fact, Alan Krueger and Pei Zhu at Princeton University obtained the raw data from Mathematica. Krueger and Zhu called the New York school voucher program "the largest and best implemented private school scholarship experiment yet conducted." But, they found that Peterson had not included 214 students who had test scores but not complete background data.[36]

Moreover, Peterson had used only the mother's ethnicity to determine race for each student. In Peterson's view, a child with a black mother and a white father was black. A child with a white mother and a black father was white. There were 78 children of mixed parentage who were considered white because their mothers were white. Krueger and Zhu thought the ethnicity of both parents should count. The two groups constituted more than 40 percent of the total sample. When Krueger and Zhu added the 214 kids with test scores but incomplete background data, and the 78 children who, by any other reckoning, would likely be considered black, the voucher impact became nil for all groups.

Mathematica's Myers weighed in again, calling Krueger's report "a fine interpretation of the results" and concluding that "the impact of a voucher offer is not statistically significant . . . It's not a study I'd want to use to make public policy."[37]

Peterson and Howell showed no such reticence. They produced a thirty-eight-page report that defended their conclusions and called a press conference at the National Press Club in

Washington, D.C. They accused Krueger and Zhu of "rummaging theoretically barefoot through data in hopes of finding desired results."[38] The Economic Policy Institute immediately set up a conference call with Krueger and other skeptics. Krueger repeated his conclusion and defended the choices he made in analyzing the data (they seem legitimate to me). Cecilia Rouse, who as we noted on page 130 had reanalyzed Peterson's Milwaukee data, said she felt uncomfortable with Peterson and Howell's conclusions.[39]

Even if the New York program had shown positive results, Moe's cautions cited on page 125 remain intact. It would be extremely risky to generalize from these small experiments about what would happen in a large-scale program.

Two other voucher studies in Dayton and Washington, D.C., also failed to find any impact of vouchers.[40] Thus, we are left with this tally:

Milwaukee: Only math favors vouchers.
New York: No advantage from vouchers.
Dayton: No advantage from vouchers.
Cleveland: No advantage from vouchers.
Washington, D.C.: No advantage from vouchers.

Moe's reservations not withstanding, it might be time to look to a different reform than vouchers.

Voucher advocates remain undeterred. In an attack on Krueger's analysis of the New York City data, Jay P. Greene (who had moved to the Manhattan Institute) looked at the evaluations from the voucher cities and concluded "None of them finds students harmed by receiving a voucher."[41] Strictly speaking, that was not true. In Dayton, in some grades, voucher students had shown losses, but the losses were not systematic and in the aggregate, the voucher students did not differ from those not using vouchers. In Cleveland, while voucher students' test scores had not declined, they had not grown as much as the scores of public school students. One could with *more* justification say that none of the evaluations found public school students harmed by *not* receiving a voucher.

Greene also showed up on a Manhattan Institute–sponsored panel to plump for Bush's proposed vouchers for the District of

Columbia (I was there to counter). For almost a year, Bush attempted to push a voucher program through Congress. Despite devious end runs of various sorts, the plan was rejected over and over again even though Senator Dianne Feinstein of California finally defected to the voucher side (but not, she said, to advocate vouchers for her state, only for D.C.) and D.C. mayor Tony Williams had been bought because the program promised millions for the public schools as well. The program finally snuck in as part of a huge omnibus spending bill in late January 2004.

The program will provide up to seventeen hundred students with vouchers worth up to $7,500. This figure, the largest ever per student, still will not buy access to the elite privates in Washington, D.C., whose tuition runs nearly three times that amount. The Catholic schools will be the prime beneficiaries and the archbishop of D.C. had earlier promised to take part in an accountability program that would involve giving the same tests in his schools as in the District of Columbia's. Edward Kennedy (D-Mass.) said, "Even after this vote, don't bank on vouchers coming to D.C."[42] We shall see.

Notes

1. Mill, John Stuart. [1838] 1991. "On Liberty." In *On Liberty and Other Essays,* 5–130. New York: Oxford University Press.

2. Dobbs, Michael. 2003. "School Choice, Limited Options." *Washington Post,* 22 December, A1.

3. Moe, Terry. 1995. *Private Vouchers.* Stanford, CA: Hoover Institution Press.

4. Richard, Alan. 2003. "Colorado Judge Puts State's Vouchers on Hold." *Education Week* (10 December).

5. Rouse, Karen. 2004. "State Court Nullifies Vouchers." *Denver Post,* 29 June, AI.

6. Miner, Barbara. 2000. "Voucher Backers Illegally Funnel Money: Wisconsin Supreme Court Race Tainted by Corruption Scandal." *Rethinking Schools* (summer): 5.

7. Witte, John F., Troy D. Sterr, and Christopher A. Thorn. 1995. *Fifth Year Report: Milwaukee Parental Choice Program.* Madison, WI: Department of Political Science, University of Wisconsin.

8. Greene, Jay P., Paul E. Peterson, and Jiangtao Du. 1996. *The Effec-*

tiveness of School Choice: The Milwaukee Experiment. Cambridge, MA: Program on Education Policy and Governance, Harvard University.

9. Greene, Jay P., and Paul E. Peterson. 1996. "Choice Data Rescued from Bad Science." *Wall Street Journal,* 14 August, 14.

10. Viadero, Debra. 2004. "In Bush Administration, Policies Drive Science, Scholars' Group Claims." *Education Week,* 3 March, 20.

11. Ibid.

12. Wakefield, Julie. 2004. "Science's Political Bulldog." *Scientific American* (May).

13. United States House of Representatives, Committee on Government Reform. 2003. *Politics and Science in the Bush Administration.* Washington, DC: United States House of Representatives. Available at *www.house .gov/reform/min/politicsandscience/pdfs/pdf_politics_and_science_rep.pdf.*

14. Wakefield, op. cit.

15. National Council for Research on Women. 2004. *Missing: Information About Women's Lives.* Washington, DC: National Council for Research on Women. Available at *www.ncrw.org/misinfo/report.pdf.*

16. Garan, Elaine M. 2002. *Resisting Reading Mandates: How to Triumph with the Truth.* Portsmouth, NH: Heinemann.

17. Allington, Richard. 2002. *Big Brother and the National Reading Curriculum.* Portsmouth, NH: Heinemann.

18. Coles, Gerald. 2003. *Reading the Naked Truth: Literacy, Legislation, and Lies.* Portsmouth, NH: Heinemann.

19. Rouse, Cecilia Elena. "School Reform in the Twenty-first Century: A Look at the Effects of Class Size and School Vouchers on the Academic Achievement of Minority Students." Working Paper #440, Industrial Relations Section. Princeton, NJ: Princeton University.

20. Nelson, Howard F. 1998. "Thirteen Ways Rouse Disagrees with GPD's Methodological Perspective." American Federation of Teachers Center on Privatization. Available at *www.aft.org/research/vouchers/mil /13ways.htm.*

21. Leovy, Jill. 2000. "School Voucher Program Teaches Hard Lessons." *Los Angeles Times,* 9 October, A1.

22. Van Dunk, Emily, and Anneliese Dickman. 2004. "The Power of School Choice Depends on Accountability." *Education Week,* 21 January, 52.

23. Brennan, David L. 1993. "Social Choice and the Educational Monopoly." *On Principle* (October): *www.ashbrook.org/publicat/onprin /vln3/brennan.html.*

24. Peterson, Paul E., Jay P. Greene, and William Howell. 1998. *An Evaluation of the Cleveland Voucher Program After Two Years.*

Cambridge, MA: Harvard University, Program in Educational Policy and Governance.

25. Bracey, Gerald W. 2002. "What Students Do in the Summer." *Phi Delta Kappan* (March): 497–98.

26. Bracey, Gerald W. 2002. "Summer Loss: The Phenomenon No One Wants to Deal With." *Phi Delta Kappan* (September): 12–13.

27. Allington, Richard, and Anne McGill-Franzen. 2003. "The Impact of Summer Setback on the Reading Achievement Gap." *Phi Delta Kappan* (September): 68–75.

28. Deloitte and Touche. 1997. *Outside Audit of the Cleveland Voucher Program.* Cleveland: Deloitte and Touche.

29. Metcalf, Kim. 2003. *Evaluation of the Cleveland Scholarship and Tutoring Program: Summary Report, 1998–2001.* Bloomington, IN: Indiana Center for Evaluation, Indiana University.

30. Ibid.

31. Oplinger, Doug, and Dennis J. Willard. 2003. "More Money for Vouchers." *Akron Beacon Journal,* 29 June, A1.

32. Howell, William G., Patrick J. Wolf, Paul E. Peterson, and David E. Campbell. 2000. "Test-Score Effects of Vouchers in Dayton, Ohio, New York City, and Washington, D.C.: Evidence from Randomized Field Trials." Available from the Program in Educational Policy and Governance, Harvard University.

33. Zernike, Kate. 2000. "New Doubt Cast on Study That Backs Voucher Efforts." *New York Times,* 15 September, A26.

34. Ibid.

35. Peterson, Paul E., and William G. Howell. 2002. *The Education Gap: Vouchers and Urban Schools.* Washington, DC: Brookings Institution.

36. Krueger, Alan B., and Pei Zhu. 2003. *Another Look at the New York City School Voucher Experiment.* Working Paper No. W9418. Princeton, NJ: National Bureau of Economic Research.

37. Winerip, Michael. 2003. "What Some Much-Noted Data Really Showed About Vouchers." *New York Times,* 7 May, B12.

38. Peterson, Paul E., and William G. Howell. 2003. "Efficiency, Bias, and Classification Schemes: Estimating Private-School Impacts on Test Scores in the New York City Voucher Experiment." Available through the Program in Education Policy and Governance, Harvard University.

39. Dillon, Sam. 2003. "A Conversation on School Vouchers." Available at *www.epinet.org/webeatures/viewpoints/vouchers_transcript_2003612.pdf.*

40. Howell, William G., Patrick J. Wolf, Paul E. Peterson, and David E. Campbell. 2000. "Test-Score Effects of Vouchers in Dayton, Ohio, New

York City, and Washington, D.C.: Evidence from Randomized Field Trials." Available from the Program in Educational Policy and Governance, Harvard University.

41. Greene, Jay P. 2003. "An Unfair Grade for Vouchers." *Wall Street Journal,* 16 May.

42. Hsu, Spencer, and Justin Blum. 2004. "D.C. Vouchers Win Final Approval." *Washington Post,* 23 January, A1.

"Dumb" Teachers

What do I say when people say, "People who go into teaching are not very bright. Certainly not as bright as those who go into other professions"?

You can say, "Actually, they are, pretty much."

This myth enjoys widespread popularity but rests largely on a single inappropriately applied statistic: high school seniors who say they are going to major in education have lower SAT scores than seniors who say they are going to major in most (but not all) other fields. For the myth to become reality, two things must happen:

1. All high school seniors who say they are going to become teachers actually become teachers.
2. No high school students who major in another field such as physics or literature become teachers.

Neither happens. Most teachers, in fact, enter from something other than an education major. In most tertiary schools, no major is declared until the end of the sophomore year, giving students over two years to reconsider the inclinations they had at the end of high school. And many students change majors, some more than once, after they get to college.

Actually, one would expect SATs for teachers to be lower than for other professions because most teachers are women and women score lower on the SAT than do men—a few points lower on the SAT verbal and about forty-five points lower on the SAT mathematics. In various college freshman math courses, in spite of the forty-five-point gender SAT differential, the women get higher grades.

Even ignoring the male-female SAT differential, we might expect would-be teachers to score lower. Schools, whether we or like it or not, sort kids. Schools encourage kids who score high on tests of all kinds to enter professions that are more prestigious or pay more or both. Given the abuse that schools have absorbed almost continuously since World War II, it is amazing that we can even come close to finding enough qualified teachers to staff the schools (we can't in math, science, and special education and in urban and rural areas). Although teacher salaries have risen slightly against inflation, the average teacher in 2002–2003 made only $47,914 a year.[1]

> *Although teacher salaries have risen slightly against inflation, the average teacher in 2002–2003 made only $47,914 a year.*

After *A Nation at Risk* appeared in 1983, it was fashionable among the political appointees in the Department of Education (although not among the career civil servants) to blame teachers for the crisis that *A Nation at Risk* allegedly revealed. Teachers, some contended, just weren't very bright. This was hardly a new charge. In the years after *Sputnik*'s launch in 1957, the grand curriculum development projects attempted to create materials that would "speak directly" to children. They would be, in other words, teacher-proof. They were, in fact, disasters.

At this time, too, some people feared that the women's movement and the civil rights movement had had a deleterious impact on the quality of teachers. Women and minorities who had previously had restricted choice of profession now found many other options. Those who had previously been confined to being nurses, for instance, could now aspire to be doctors; those who could approach the bar only as a legal secretary could now go to law school.

The Education Department's Office of Planning, Budget, and Evaluation commissioned independent researcher John Lee to document this widely known "fact." Unfortunately for the department, the fact failed to materialize.[2] Using a large national database, the study examined a number of variables, of which the one with the most direct bearing on the teachers-are-dumb situation was the grade point average of students at the end of their sophomore year in college. At this point in their college careers, those intending to major in education would not yet have taken any of those gut education courses in which everyone supposedly gets As. Those who intended to teach had an average GPA of 2.88 while those who intended to major in something else had an average GPA of 2.87. At the end of the senior year, future teachers had an average GPA of 3.05 and those in other fields, an average GPA of 2.95. Neither of these senior figures smacks of rampant grade inflation in education or elsewhere.

When the needed fact failed to appear, the study got buried in the bowels of the Department of Education. I learned of its existence from an offhand remark by David Imig of American Association of Colleges on Teacher Education (AACTE) some twelve years later. Contacted by phone, Lee said, "We made a presentation to the department. It didn't go over very well with the political appointees." Fortunately, Dan Morrisey, the department's program officer for the research, placed the study in the ERIC system, from which I was able to retrieve it.

More recently, researchers at the Educational Testing Service used data from the U.S. Department of Education's National Adult Literacy Survey (NALS) to compare actual teachers' literacy skills with those of other groups: the general public, those with a bachelor's degree, and those in other professional and managerial positions.[3] NALS defines three literacies: prose, document, and quantitative. All involve extracting information from text and, in the quantitative section, manipulating it in some arithmetical fashion. The three are highly correlated, but a given person often does better in one than the others. NALS investigators converted the scores into a five-point scale with 1 being the lowest and 5 the highest. People who score at the first level are not necessarily "functionally illiterate" (whatever that means). According to NALS, they can do simple tasks with text and few of them report that their literacy lacks cause them problems in their lives.

About 75 percent of teachers scored at levels 3 and 4 and another 12 percent scored at level 5 (there were small differences among prose, document, and quantitative literacy). This compares with 49 percent and 3 percent, respectively, in the general populace. This is not the best comparison, of course, because virtually all teachers have at least a bachelor's degree and only about

25 percent of the population as a whole has attained that level of education.

When compared with other people with a bachelor's degree, teachers still fared well. Their scores were virtually identical to other college-educated people on all three literacies. Similarly, when teachers with advanced degrees were compared with other professions, the scores on all three literacies were quite similar. In terms of levels, 82 percent of teachers scored at levels 3 or 4 and 13 percent scored at level 5. This compares with 75 percent and 16 percent, respectively, in other professions. When the researchers compared teachers' scores with the scores of specific professional groups, seven groups scored significantly higher and eight scored significantly lower than teachers.

It is worth noting that higher test scores have a bigger payoff in other occupations than in teaching. While teachers scoring at level 5 earned more than those scoring at level 4, who in turn outearned those at level 3, the differentials for teachers were much smaller than in other fields.

It is worth noting that higher test scores have a bigger payoff in other occupations than in teaching.

Yet another study looked at various indicators of new college graduates who actually became teachers and those who didn't. The general conclusion: "On several of the characteristics examined—including gender, college entrance examination scores, cumulative GPAs, or major GPAs, and credits earned in advanced mathematics or calculus—secondary school teachers did not differ from their classmates who had not entered the teacher pipeline. Thus the differences between teachers and those outside the pipeline represented differences between elementary school teachers and those outside the pipeline."[4]

This study thus indicates that those who are heading for elementary teaching positions don't score as well on the SAT and don't get as high grades in college as those heading for secondary schools. This raises the question What does an elementary teacher need to know? What level of knowledge does it take to be a competent teacher in elementary school? The conventional wisdom is that elementary teachers teach kids and secondary teachers teach subjects. This, if true, and I think it is, means that elementary teachers need to be sensitive to a whole range of student characteristics besides academic prowess (see page 32 for a list of personal qualities that test scores do not measure).

We might want, of course, there to be a difference in SATs and GPAs between teachers and others, in favor of the teachers. Until the conditions of teaching change rather drastically, that is not likely to happen.

Notes

1. National Education Association. 2003. *Rankings and Estimates, 2003.* Washington, DC: National Education Association.

2. Lee, John. 1984. *Tomorrow's Teachers.* ERIC Document ED 263 042. October.

3. Bruschi, Barbara A., and Richard J. Coley. 1999. *How Teachers Compare: The Prose, Document and Quantitative Skills of America's Teachers.* Princeton, NJ: Policy Information Center, Educational Testing Service.

4. Henke, Robin R., Sonya Geis, and Jennifer Giammbatista. 1996. *Out of the Lecture Hall and into the Classroom: 1992–93 College Graduates and Elementary/Secondary School Teaching.* Washington, DC: National Center for Education Statistics.

⚡ Rising Costs, Flat Scores

What do I say when someone says, "During the 1980s, expenditures for public education rose by 34 percent (in real dollars), but test scores were static"? Or when someone says, "In the last twenty-five years, spending on public schools has risen by 100 percent, but test scores are flat"?

You can reply with the following points:
1. *Spending has not risen nearly as much as critics contend.*
2. *A great deal of increased spending has gone to special education and other special populations. We would have little reason to expect increases in test scores from such increases in spending.*
3. *Many test scores have risen since the mid-1970s and some are at record highs.*
4. *Gains in test scores are often obscured by the way in which they are reported. (Really. This is not just an example of how to lie with statistics.)*

1. Spending.

The first of the quotes in the opening paragraph is from Denis Doyle, who said it as a Hudson Institute consultant in 1992 and repeated it in 1994 in a book he coauthored (wrote, actually) with then RJR Nabisco CEO Louis V. Gerstner (by publication time, Gerstner was CEO at IBM). The second statement was made in 1994, and often repeated since, by both Eric Hanushek and Chester E. Finn Jr., at a Brookings Institution luncheon launching a Hanushek book.

People who allege that school spending doubled in twenty-five years use the consumer price index (CPI) to calculate inflation. Using the CPI does lead to the perception that costs have increased greatly, particularly in a twenty-five-year period that includes the 1970s and 1980s. We don't hear this "spending has doubled" argument too much these days because inflation was tame in the 1990s and in the early years of the twenty-first century.

Using the CPI is inappropriate, however, to calculate increases in school spending. The CPI is useful for changes in the net prices of *commodities* but much less so in calculating changes in *services,* especially for the kinds of services rendered by schools. Richard Rothstein and Karen Hawley Miles argue for the use of a more appropriate index based on labor-intensive, slow-productivity growth industries.[1] Business and industry have realized large productivity gains through changes in technology, especially information technology.

Schools, though, more closely resemble a symphony orchestra than they resemble some product industry. How can a symphony orchestra increase productivity? It cannot do so by playing the music faster or by playing with fewer players than the score calls for. Schools could play with fewer players, by increasing the pupil–teacher ratios, but this change is associated with *decreased* productivity in terms of pupil achievement. At this time, high-stakes testing programs are attempting to increase "productivity" by decreasing the number of products created, that is, by reducing the range of the curriculum to cover only what is found on the tests. This does not appear to be working and is accompanied by what the military would call collateral damage: increased dropouts, increased anxiety, teacher retirements, loss of teachers to other fields, and in a few cases, student suicides.

Rothstein and Miles found that between 1967 and 1991, spending for education had increased by 67 percent, an increase of 2 percent per year, far less than the critics claimed.[2] In a follow-up, Rothstein found that from 1991 to 1996, spending on education increased only .7 percent per year.[3]

2. Where Does the Money Go?

Schools perform many services, not all of them related to improving test scores. To determine if schools are inefficient, we need to look at where the money is going. As Rothstein and Miles put it,

> To understand school spending and to determine whether school productivity is truly declining (i.e., whether additional

dollars have been well used), expenditures must be linked to the program and to the specific outcomes the spending was designed to enhance. If, for example, schools have used much of their new money to improve the training of mentally handicapped youngsters, it would make no sense to judge the effectiveness of this spending by whether SAT scores improved for the college bound. (8)

So where does the money go? The short answer is, it goes to special education. Several studies reveal this at both the state and the national levels. Hamilton Lankford and James Wyckoff examined the issue for the state of New York.[4] They found that in 1980, special education accounted for 5.9 percent of school expenditures. By 1992, special education's share had soared to 13.1 percent, a 122 percent increase. Similarly, an analysis of New Mexico's spending found that from 1976 to 1990, regular education costs had increased by 8 percent while special education costs had sky-rocketed by 340 percent (281).[5]

> *Schools perform many services, not all of them related to improving test scores. To determine if schools are inefficient, we need to look at where the money is going.*

At the national level, Rothstein and Miles uncovered similar trends. In 1967, special education received only 4 percent of all spending, but by 1991 it received 18 percent, four and a half times the 1967 amount. Other increases went for dropout programs and meals programs. Regular education got less than a quarter of the 1967–1991 increases. In his 1997 follow-up, Rothstein found special education costs climbing to 19 percent of all expenditures.[6] School lunch and breakfast programs grew from 3.3 percent in 1991 to 4.8 percent in 1996, while bilingual education costs grew from 1.9 percent in 1991 to 2.5 percent in 1996. Regular education expenses dropped from 58.5 percent in 1991 to 56.8 percent in 1996. None of these allocations could be expected to bring dramatic increases in test scores.

3. Flat Test Scores.

When people hear someone say, "Test scores are flat," they would do well to ask, "What test scores are you talking about?" Some claimants, such as Doyle, will then specify the SAT. This isn't true, but at least we know what he has in mind. Readers will find that Hanushek means only the NAEP reading scores for seventeen-year-olds. This isn't true, either, but at least we know that Hanushek is *not* referring to NAEP science or math scores for seventeen-year-olds or any scores for nine- and thirteen-year-olds, which clearly contradict his assertion.

We will deal with NAEP and SAT scores in the next section. For the moment, let's concentrate on the outcomes for the only standardized achievement test for which we have long-term data, the Iowa Tests of Basic Skills (grades 3–8) and the Iowa Tests of Educational Development (grades 9–12). By Iowa law, each new version of these tests must be equated to the earlier version, permitting, as with the SAT, long-term comparisons. The ITBS and ITED were qualitatively revised in 1955, so our data begin there. In addition, the scale on the ITED was changed in 1993, making prior comparisons iffy, as there is no formula for conversion. The trends for the ITED show the same patterns, though, as do those for the ITBS, which are shown in Figure 11–1 from 1955 through 2000. We see that there was no decline in the earliest grades, but in the upper elementary grades and middle school grades, scores rise from roughly 1955 to 1965, decline from 1965 to roughly 1975, then rise again *to record high scores* (the ITED shows the same pattern as the middle grades of the ITBS). The lowest grades have also been affected by the decline seen in the 2000 norms.

On pages 56 and 57, I discussed the many social upheavals of the mid-1960s to mid-1970s. Given the turmoil in the culture at large, and its antiacademic cast, it would have been a *miracle* (and very suspicious) if test scores had *not* declined. But about the same time that the Vietnam War ended, scores started to rise, reaching record levels in the mid- to late 1980s. They have since declined some, although they remain substantially above the low levels of the 1970s.

No one has a complete explanation for this latest decline. My candidate for the leading factor is immigration. Hispanics are now the largest minority group in the nation and many do not speak English as a native language. In addition, immigrants come from many other nations. In Fairfax County, Virginia, where I live, the

Iowa Tests of Basic Skills National Norming Data Trends, 1955–2000 in Grade Equivalents						
	1955	1963	1970	1977	1984	1992	2000
Grade 3	3.2	3.4	3.4	3.7	3.9	4.0	3.8
Grade 4	4.2	4.4	4.4	4.3	4.6	4.8	4.6
Grade 5	5.2	5.4	5.4	5.2	5.6	5.9	5.7
Grade 6	6.1	6.3	6.2	6.1	6.5	6.8	6.6
Grade 7	7.1	7.3	7.2	7.0	7.5	7.6	7.5
Grade 8	8.2	8.3	8.2	7.7	8.3	8.4	8.3

Source: Riverside Publishing Company and Iowa Testing Programs, University of Iowa

Figure 11–1. Iowa Tests of Basic Schools

schools must cope with 105 languages other than English. And these nonnative English speakers must try to cope with tests.

Tests try to trick people into picking the wrong answer and to do that, the language is often subtle. If the test items could not trick people into choosing wrong answers, they would not be on the test. For a test to "behave" properly, test takers must, on average, get only about 50 percent of the items right. Students who can competently converse in English or even perform well in class (where there are many other ways of being understood than just picking one of four preselected choices) might well get tripped up on the deceptive syntax of a standardized test.

It is important to note that scores likely did not decline each year from 1992 to 2000, although that appears to be the case in Figure 11–1. The graph, though, consists of national results for years when the test was revised and renormed. The Iowas are given in Iowa every year and there is no indication of any decline on these annual tests until about 1997. The decline in Iowa has apparently leveled off.

It is also important to note that for most grades the scores are substantially above where they were in 1955 or at the nadir year of 1977.

4. Deceptive Reporting of SATs and NAEP Scores. These Trends Are Not Flat— Simpson's Paradox Explained.

The people who take the SAT constitute a self-selecting group of seniors intending to attend four-year colleges. The kids who sit for NAEP constitute a national probability sample. Nevertheless, the demographics of both groups have changed dramatically over the years. This means that an average score from 2003 cannot be meaningfully compared with an average score from twenty or thirty years earlier. Both tests are taken increasingly by groups whose scores are improving—blacks and Hispanics—but whose scores remain below those of whites and Asians. When all scores are lumped together to report one national average score, the increasing proportion of these low but improving students attenuates the national average. This phenomenon is common in research, so common it has a name: Simpson's Paradox. It appears when the total sample shows one pattern and a subgroup shows another (see Figure 11–2).

Assume the 500s at Time 1 represent the SAT scores of white students. Assume the 400 at Time 1 represents SAT scores of minorities. When we average these scores, we find the mean to be 490.

Now, assume the 510s at Time 2 represent the SAT scores of white students and assume the 430s at Time 2 represent SAT scores of minorities. The average score for Time 2 is 486.

Thus, from Time 1 to Time 2, the scores of white students have improved (500 to 510). The scores of minorities have improved, and have improved substantially more than the improvement seen for white students (400 to 430). But, the scores for minorities still fall below those of white students. And, most importantly, at Time 1, minorities made up 10 percent of the total sample, but at Time 2, they constituted 30 percent of the total. When we find the average for everyone at Time 2, even though white and minority scores have improved, the average has actually *declined* from Time 1 to Time 2, from 490 to 486. This is Simpson's Paradox: individual groups show one pattern, the aggregate shows another.

Obviously, a declining average created by adding more low scorers means something different than a declining average created by all scores falling.

Time 1	Time 2
500	510
500	510
500	510
500	510
500	510
500	510
500	510
500	430
500	430
400	430
———	———
490	486

Figure 11–2. Simpson's Paradox Explained

This is essentially what has happened in the United States over the last twenty years—the proportion of minorities has grown substantially and their test scores have improved, but the scores remain, for most groups, below the average scores of whites. We start in 1981 because that was the first year the College Board published reports of SAT scores by ethnicity.[7] Consider the following numbers using the ethnic categories of the College Board:

Ethnic Makeup of
SAT Test-Taking Pool, 1981–2003

	1981	2003
White	85	64
Black	9	12
Asian	3	10
Mexican	2	5
Puerto Rican	1	1
American Indian	0	1

The percentages for 2003 do not sum to 100 percent because 4 percent chose "other" and another 4 percent picked "Latino." Neither option was available in 1981. If these were added in, the sum would be 101 percent, a figure that stems from rounding.

The 1981–2003 comparisons show a dramatic shift in the ethnic makeup of the test-taking sample. What does this do to the score? The national average SAT verbal score[8] in 1981 was 504 and in 2003 it was 507 (in 2002 it was still 504). Virtually no gain. But all ethnic groups showed increases:

Gains for Ethnic Groups—Verbal

	1981	2003	Gain
Whites	519	529	10
Blacks	412	431	19
Asians	474	508	34
Mexicans	438	448	10
Puerto Ricans	437	456	19
American Indians	471	480	9
All Groups	504	507	3

> *Thus, every ethnic group increased over a twenty-year period, but taken together, the country showed virtually no change. Simpson's Paradox strikes again.*

Thus, every ethnic group increased over a twenty-year period, but taken together, the country showed virtually no change. Simpson's Paradox strikes again.

The SAT math shows a similar pattern. From 1981 to 2003, the national average went from 494 to 519, a gain of twenty-five points. But whites gained twenty-five points, blacks thirty-seven, and Asians sixty-three.

Simpson's Paradox also affects NAEP trends. Figure 11–3 shows the overall NAEP trends in reading, math, and science from NAEP's inception through 1999. Of the nine trendlines, only the math scores of nine- and thirteen-year-olds are not flat.

Again, though, the nation's changing ethnic makeup obscured the gains. Figure 11–4 shows the reading scores for blacks, whites, and Hispanics (other ethnic groups were not large enough to generate reliable estimates of scores). For whites, scores were up somewhat at all three ages. For blacks and Hispanics, the scores were up a lot.

For mathematics, again scores for whites were up somewhat and up substantially for blacks and Hispanics. For science, whites'

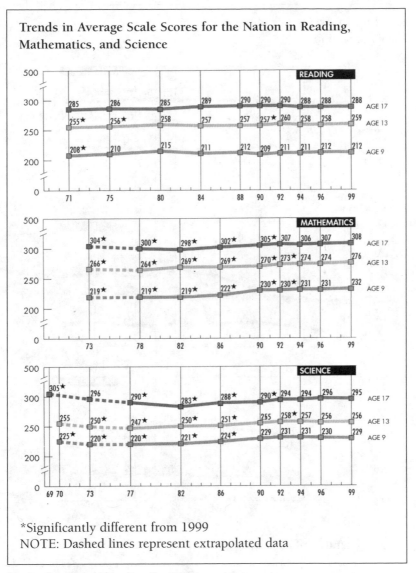

Figure 11–3. Trends—Reading, Math, and Science

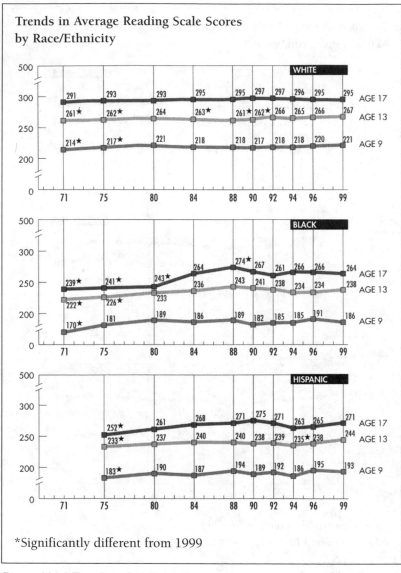

Figure 11–4. Trends in Reading—Race

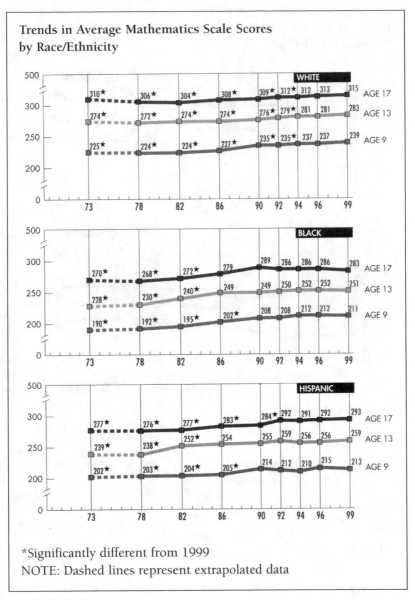

Trends in Average Mathematics Scale Scores
by Race/Ethnicity

*Significantly different from 1999
NOTE: Dashed lines represent extrapolated data

Figure 11–5. Trends in Math—Race

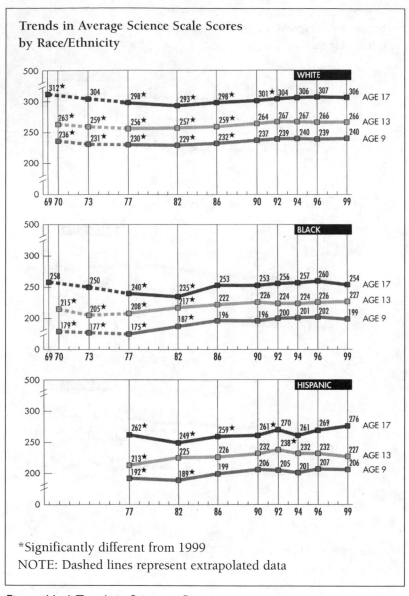

Trends in Average Science Scale Scores
by Race/Ethnicity

*Significantly different from 1999
NOTE: Dashed lines represent extrapolated data

Figure 11–6. Trends in Science—Race

scores were indeed pretty flat, as they were for blacks at age seventeen. For nine- and thirteen-year-old blacks and for Hispanics of all ages, scores were up. These trends are shown in Figures 11–5 and 11–6, respectively.

Thus we see that for both the SAT and the NAEP, while there is little shift in the aggregate average for the nation as a whole, every ethnic group taking the tests has shown improvement—in some instances, dramatic improvement.

A Few Important Notes on NAEP Trends

1. There are two NAEP programs: the trend analysis and what NAEP calls its "main" analysis. Assessments for the trend analysis cover pretty much the same material from time to time. The main assessments change according to what is current in curriculum. Trends are analyzed by age, main assessments by grade. The two assessments are not comparable and do not always paint the same picture. For instance, in the decade from 1990 to 2000, scores rose substantially on the main NAEP mathematics assessment, but only slightly in the trend analysis. Tom Loveless at the Brookings Institution worried that the rise in the main NAEP but not the trend reflected the adoption of National Council of Teachers of Mathematics standards by both NAEP and schools. These standards do not emphasize the traditional computational skills reflected in the older trend assessments.[9] I'd call that a stretch.

2. The broken lines in the analysis are not "real" data. NAEP originally was not designed to produce trends. The broken lines are backward extrapolations. Items common to the first trend assessment and earlier assessments were used to calculate the results. In all instances, trends would show larger gains using only real data. This consistency could lead one to think there might be some sort of bias in the extrapolations. However, since the extrapolations are to periods where other test scores were falling, they might well be accurate representations.

3. Data for Hispanics began in the mid-1970s as this ethnic group grew large enough to generate a reliable outcome. Although NAEP reported Asian data for the 1996 science assess-

ment and the 2000 mathematics assessment, NAEP analysts still worry that the estimates might not be reliable because of small sample sizes or sampling inaccuracies.

Notes

1. Rothstein, Richard, and Karen Hawley Miles. 1995. *Where Has the Money Gone?* Washington, DC: Economic Policy Institute.

2. Ibid.

3. Rothstein, Richard. 1997. *Where's the Money Going?* Washington, DC: Economic Policy Institute.

4. Lankford, Hamilton, and James Wyckoff. 1995. "Where Has the Money Gone?" *Educational Evaluation and Policy Analysis* (summer): 195–218.

5. Carson, C. C., R. M. Huelskamp, and T. D. Woodall. 1993. "Perspectives on Education in America." *Journal of Educational Research* (May/June): 249–311.

6. Rothstein, op. cit.

7. All scores in this analysis have been placed on the recentered SAT score and so can be directly compared across the years (see "The Notorious 1995 SAT 'Recentering,'" page 57).

8. There is no real national average for the SAT or the ACT. This is because the proportion of seniors taking these tests varies enormously from state to state. Some eastern states have almost 80 percent of their seniors take the SAT, some southern and western states have only 4 percent.

9. Loveless, Tom. 2002. *The Brown Center Report on American Education: How Well Are American Students Learning?* Washington, DC: Brookings Institution.

12 International Comparisons

What do I say when people say, "American kids just can't keep up with their peers in other countries"?

You can say, "They do anywhere from average to well above average. And it looks like test scores don't have much to do with anything we might call global competitiveness."

Many of the data from the various international comparisons have been worked in as answers to other queries. These comparisons appear as follows:

Third International Mathematics and Science Study, 1996–2000 (TIMSS): pages 15–26
Program of International Student Assessment (PISA), 2001: pages 26–29
Progress in International Reading Literacy Study (PIRLS), 2003, and poverty: page 50
PISA and poverty: page 51

Here I summarize findings from TIMSS and PISA and present more data from the International Association for the Evaluation of Educational Achievement (IEA) reading study and from PIRLS.

In TIMSS, American fourth graders scored above average in math and ranked third in the world in science among the twenty-six participating nations. At the eighth grade, American students were tied for seventeenth place in science and twenty-seventh in math, with forty-one countries participating. In the TIMSS Final

Year of Secondary School report, American twelfth graders appeared to be at or near the bottom, but as we have seen (pages 21–25), the operative word is *appeared*. Those American twelfth graders who were most like their peers abroad remained in the middle of the pack.

However, ranks are somewhat misleading in this context, especially if we use percent correct rather than the scaled scores that generated the ranks just mentioned. Consider the various average percent correct scores in science at the eighth grade, shown in Figure 12–1.

While a few Asian nations are clearly above most nations and while a few Third World nations are well below most, note how closely most countries bunch up. The United States' exact score is shared by six other nations. If Americans had managed to get a mere 5 percent more correct, they'd have jumped up all the way to fifth place. Conversely, if they had gotten a mere 5 percent fewer correct, they'd have fallen all the way to twenty-ninth.

> *Ranks by their very nature can make small differences in scores seem big.*

Ranks by their very nature can make small differences in scores seem big. When they run the final heat of the Olympic one-hundred-meter dash, someone will rank last. He will be close to the other seven, will still be the eighth fastest human being on the planet at that distance, and will probably not be referred to by his peers as "Pokey."

Now it is true that some small differences in scores make huge differences in payoff. Sticking with the Olympics for the moment, we know that in some events, the difference between a gold medal and a silver has been one–one hundredth of a second. Small differences had huge consequences in the 2000 presidential election. I cannot imagine, though, that a few percent correct on a paper-and-pencil test has much bearing on anything in the practical world or in the future.

The earlier IEA reading study was conducted in 1991 and published in 1992 as *How in the World Do Students Read?* The study tested ten-year-olds in twenty-seven nations and fourteen-year-olds in thirty-one.

Separate scores were reported for narrative passages, expository passages, documents, and overall performances. Differences among the three types of literacy were mostly small and where

Average Percent Correct
TIMSS Eighth-Grade Science

1.	Singapore	70	22.	Hong Kong	58
2.	Korea	66	23.	Israel	57
3.	Japan	65	24.	Thailand	57
4.	Czech Republic	64	25.	Switzerland	56
5.	Bulgaria	62	26.	Spain	56
6.	Slovenia	62	27.	Scotland	55
7.	Netherlands	62	28.	France	54
8.	England	61	29.	Iceland	52
9.	Hungary	61	30.	Greece	52
10.	Austria	61	31.	Denmark	51
11.	Belgium	60	32.	Latvia	50
12.	Australia	60	33.	Portugal	50
13.	Slovak Republic	59	34.	Romania	50
14.	Sweden	59	35.	Belgium (French)	50
15.	Canada	59	36.	Lithuania	49
16.	Ireland	58	37.	Iran	47
17.	United States	58	38.	Cyprus	47
18.	Russian Federation	58	39.	Kuwait	43
19.	New Zealand	58	40.	Colombia	39
20.	Germany	58	41.	South Africa	27
21.	Norway	58			

Figure 12–1. Average Percent Correct TIMSS Eighth-Grade Science

they were large, they were probably of interest only to the country involved. For instance, Hong Kong students had a substantially higher expository score (540) than narrative (509) and a higher document score still (557). Since these students took the test in English, it is plausible that the subtleties of fiction might well have been harder for them to handle than the more straightforward prose of expository passages and documents. Conversely, American students scored slightly lower on documents (528) than on narrative and exposition (539 on both). Observers have noted that American schools concentrate on literature, perhaps to the detriment of reading technical material. The average scores are shown in Figure 12–2.

As can be seen, American ten-year-olds finished second while

Ten-Year-Olds		Fourteen-Year-Olds	
1. Finland	569	1. Finland	560
2. United States	547	2. France	549
3. Sweden	539	3. Sweden	546
4. France	531	4. New Zealand	545
5. Italy	529	5. Hungary	536
6. New Zealand	528	6. Iceland	536
7. Norway	524	7. Switzerland	536
8. Iceland	518	8. United States	535
9. Hong Kong*	527	9. Hong Kong*	535
10. Singapore*	515	10. Singapore*	534
11. Switzerland	511	11. Slovenia	532
12. Ireland	509	12. East Germany	526
13. Belgium (French)	507	13. Denmark	525
14. Greece	504	14. Portugal	523
15. Spain	504	15. Canada‡	522
16. West Germany	503	16. West Germany	522
17. Canada‡	500	17. Norway	516
18. East Germany	499	18. Italy	515
19. Hungary	499	19. Netherlands	514
20. Slovenia	498	20. Ireland	511
21. Netherlands	485	21. Greece	509
22. Cyprus	481	22. Cyprus	497
23. Portugal	478	23. Spain	490
24. Denmark	475	24. Belgium (French)	481
25. Trinidad/Tobago	451	25. Trinidad/Tobago	479
26. Indonesia	394	26. Thailand	477
27. Venezuela	383	27. Philippines	430
		28. Venezuela	417
		29. Nigeria	401
		30. Zimbabwe	372
		31. Botswana	330

*Took the tests in English
‡ Only British Columbia took part

Figure 12–2. IEA Reading Scores

fourteen-year-olds tied for eighth with Hong Kong. However, as with TIMSS, ranks and scores paint different pictures. The scores of the fourteen-year-olds were more tightly bunched than those of

1.	Sweden	561	19.	Greece	524
2.	Netherlands	554	20.	Slovak Republic	518
3.	England	553	21.	Iceland	512
4.	Bulgaria	550	22.	Romania	512
5.	Latvia	545	23.	Israel	509
6.	Canada‡	544	24.	Slovenia	502
7.	Lithuania	543	25.	Norway	499
8.	Hungary	543	26.	Cyprus	494
9.	United States	542	27.	Moldova	492
10.	Italy	541	28.	Turkey	449
11.	Germany	539	29.	Macedonia	442
12.	Czech Republic	537	30.	Colombia	422
13.	New Zealand	529	31.	Argentina	420
14.	Scotland	528	32.	Iran	419
15.	Singapore*	528	33.	Kuwait	396
16.	Russian Federation	528	34.	Morocco	350
17.	Hong Kong*	528	35.	Belize	327
18.	France	525			

*Took the tests in English
‡ Only British Columbia took part

Figure 12–3. PIRLS Average Scores

the nine-year-olds, meaning that small differences in scores would produce differences in ranks among the fourteen-year-olds.

Thus we see that the American nine-year-olds are twenty-two points out of first place. The fourteen-year-olds are twenty-five points away from first, virtually the same distance. Only Finland has a score that is statistically significantly higher than the U.S. at both ages.

At both ages America's best readers outscored even Finland's best. That is, the scores of American students scoring at the United States' ninetieth, ninety-fifth, and ninety-ninth percentiles were higher than the scores of Finnish students with those ranks in Finland. The differences are tiny, though, and certainly not statistically significant, much less practically important.

IEA came back in 2001 with PIRLS, this time testing only ten-year-olds in thirty-five countries. American students finished ninth overall, but only three countries had significantly higher

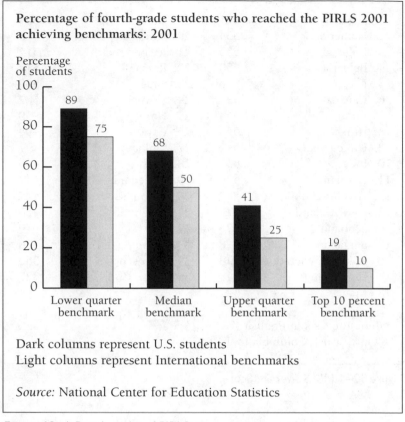

Percentage of fourth-grade students who reached the PIRLS 2001 achieving benchmarks: 2001

Dark columns represent U.S. students
Light columns represent International benchmarks

Source: National Center for Education Statistics

Figure 12–4. Benchmarks of PIRLS

scores. The overall reading score was composed of separate prose and information items. On the prose items, American students finished third and only one country had a significantly higher score, while on the information scale, American students finished twelfth and five nations had significantly higher scores. Figure 12–3 shows the average scores.

The scores on PIRLS are a bit more spread out than on TIMSS or PISA because, as one can see by looking at the bottom of the list, there are more developing nations in PIRLS than in the earlier IEA study. Developed nations, though, have mostly similar scores. Indeed, one might think that to be called a developed nation requires that the country have a mature educational system in place for some time.

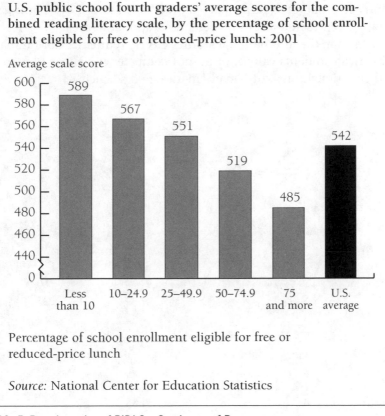

U.S. public school fourth graders' average scores for the combined reading literacy scale, by the percentage of school enrollment eligible for free or reduced-price lunch: 2001

Average scale score

Percentage of school enrollment eligible for free or reduced-price lunch

Source: National Center for Education Statistics

12–5. Benchmarks of PIRLS—Students of Poverty

At all of the benchmarks of PIRLS, Americans had a higher percentage of students scoring at or above the benchmark than overall. For instance, by definition, 10 percent of the students scored at or above the ninetieth percentile. Some 19 percent of American students scored at or above the score that constituted the ninetieth percentile for all students. The benchmark performance of American students is shown in Figure 12–4.

> *At all of the benchmarks of PIRLS, Americans had a higher percentage of students scoring at or above the benchmark than overall.*

I noted on page 50 that American students in schools with fewer than 25 percent of the students living in poverty outscored the highest nation and the students in schools with fewer than 50 percent of their students in poverty outscored all but three of the thirty-five nations taking part in PIRLS. Figure 12–5 shows a graphic representation of those and additional figures.

In sum, the international studies clearly refute the notion that American students cannot or do not compete with those of many other nations in reading, mathematics, and science.

13 Knowledge Nostalgia
The Dumbing of America?

What do I say when someone says, "Kids don't know as much as they used to"?

You can say, "Yes they do. And for some indicators they clearly know more."

As noted in the introduction, shortly after World War II there arose the notion that at some time in the past everyone learned and learned well. Arthur Bestor titled his 1953 book, *Educational Wastelands: The Retreat from Learning in the Public Schools* (emphasis added). More recently, Terrel Bell, secretary of education in the Reagan administration, wrote:

> If we are frank with ourselves, we must acknowledge that for most Americans, neither diligence in learning nor rigorous standards of performance prevail . . . How do we *once again become a nation of learners*, in which attitudes toward intellectual pursuit and quality of work have excellence at their core. (167, emphasis added)[1]

On the other hand, in his too-little-read book, *Popular Education and Its Discontents*, education historian Laurence Cremin looked back in perplexity:

> The popularization of American schools and colleges since the end of World War II has been nothing short of phenomenal, involving an unprecedented broadening of access, an unprecedented diversification of curricula, and an unprecedented extension of public control. In 1950, 34 percent of the

169

American population twenty-five years of age or older had completed at least four years of high school, while 6 percent of that population completed four years of college. By 1985, 74 percent of the American population twenty-five years or older had completed at least four years of high school, while 19 percent had completed at least four years of college.

Yet this [expansion of schooling] seemed to bring with it a pervasive sense of failure. The question would have to be "Why?" (40–41)[2]

Why, indeed?

This idea that there was some glorious golden age of American education from which we have deteriorated has been abetted and sustained by surveys, accompanied by the clucking of tongues, alleging that students cannot find X country on the map. In the 1990s, it was Mexico and Canada, in the early part of the twenty-first century, it's Afghanistan and Iraq.

Anecdotes also sustain the myth. Former Assistant Secretary of Education Chester E. Finn Jr. begins his book *We Must Take Charge* with a sad tale of ignoramuses sharing his flight from Minneapolis to Frankfurt. They don't know whether they gain or lose time en route and one says it's the first time he's ever flown over the Pacific. Cluck, cluck. Anecdotes can be matched, of course. I had an uncle who resisted daylight savings time on the grounds that God's time was good enough for him.

Ralph Tyler, who rose to prominence in the Eight Year Study (1933–1941) and later became the father of the National Assessment of Educational Progress and one of our wisest and most long-lived educators, reflected on his own experiences in 1976, when he was a mere pup of seventy-four (he died in 1993):

> What I remember of my experience as a pupil are the strictness of discipline, the catechismic type of recitation, the dullness of the textbooks, and the complete absence of any obvious connection between our classwork and the activities we carried on outside of school . . . The view held by most teachers and parents was that the school was quite separate from the other institutions in society and its tasks should be sufficiently distasteful to the pupils to require strong discipline to undertake them and carry them through. Furthermore, they believed that while school children should not talk with one another, all communi-

cation should be between the teacher and the class as a whole or between the teacher and the individual. (26)[3]

Tyler's words echoed those of the Committee of Ten (so called because it was made up of five college presidents and five school superintendents) appointed in 1892 by the National Educational Association to establish a standard curriculum. The committee's report leaves one wondering just what students in high school did all day:

> As things are now, the high school teacher finds in the pupils from the grammar schools no foundation of elementary mathematical conceptions outside of arithmetic, no acquaintance with algebraic language, and no accurate knowledge of geometrical forms. As to botany, zoology, chemistry, and physics, the minds of pupils entering the high school are ordinarily blank on these subjects. When college professors endeavor to teach chemistry, physics, botany, zoology, meteorology or geology to persons of eighteen or twenty years of age, they discover that in most instances new habits of observing, reflecting, and recording have to be painfully acquired—habits which they should have acquired in early childhood. The college teacher of history finds in like manner that his subject has never taken any serious hold on the minds of pupils fresh from secondary schools.[4]

Fifty years after the Committee of Ten's report, things didn't look much better:

> A large majority of the students showed that they had virtually no knowledge of elementary aspects of American history. They could not identify such names as Abraham Lincoln, Thomas Jefferson, Andrew Jackson or Theodore Roosevelt . . . Most of the students do not have the faintest notion of what this country looks like. St. Louis was placed on the Pacific Ocean, Lake Huron, Lake Erie, the Atlantic Ocean, Ohio River, St. Laurence River and almost everyplace else.[5]

This was the conclusion of the *New York Times,* which had commissioned the history department at Columbia University to conduct a survey. The results incensed the *Times* and the paper headlined the story on page 1 of a Sunday edition next to its featured headline of the day, "Patton Attacks East of El Guettar," on April 4, 1943.

Asked to identify Walt Whitman, students created many occupations; "Hundreds of students thought Walt Whitman was a bandleader." The *Times* did not see the connection to Paul Whiteman, a popular jazz band leader of the day (George Gershwin wrote "Rhapsody in Blue" for Whiteman's orchestra).

The *Times* also did not comment on what was surely the most damning aspect of its findings: it had surveyed college freshman. At the time, the high school graduation rate ran close to 45 percent. Of those, some 15 percent went on to college. So the *Times* survey covered the elite 7 percent (45 x .15) of the presumably most academically able in the nation.

Even at the height of the Cold War, Americans knew little about the enemy that threatened them with annihilation. Harrison Salisbury surveyed college graduates and found that only 71 percent knew that Moscow was Russia's capital; only 21 percent could name a single Russian author; and only 24 percent could name a single Russian composer. I suppose it is possible that, in these the days of the McCarthy witch-hunts for communists, the respondents might have feared that knowledge of the Soviet Union could be taken as leftist leanings, but I doubt it.

The myth of decline gained additional credibility in 1977 with the release of *On Further Examination,* the report of a panel appointed by the College Board to study what was then a fourteen-year decline in average SAT scores. This report was discussed at length on pages 56–57. Suffice it to repeat here that the panel found a host of causes for the decline, most of which were outside of the schools. The media and the public had a simpler interpretation: the schools, the high schools at least, were failing.

In modern times, *A Nation at Risk* gave the myth additional strength, and it received another boost by Finn and fellow traveler Diane Ravitch in their book on student knowledge of history and literature, *What Do Our Seventeen-Year-Olds Know?*[6] Their answer was not much: "If there were such a thing as a national report card for those studying American history and literature, then we would have to say that this nationally representative sample of 11th-grade students earns failing marks in both subjects" (1).

The myth is also sustained by the differential media attention to good and bad news. We saw on page xii how the media largely ignored a positive NAEP geography report but jumped all over a less than stellar history report.

To say that we were ignorant then and things worked out pretty well is not to say it's OK to be ignorant now. This is not the Forrest Gump defense of public schools. However, much of the data I have presented thus far in this book makes it obvious that students do know more now and that they know enough to compete well with peers in other developed nations.

> *To say that we were ignorant then and things worked out pretty well is not to say it's OK to be ignorant now. This is not the Forrest Gump defense of public schools.*

Even in the areas that Finn and Ravitch attacked, an empirical attempt to figure out what people knew in the past finds no superiority in past generations. Dale Whittington gathered test data from 1917, 1933, 1944, and 1964. She matched the content of these assessments with those used by Finn and Ravitch. She concluded "students of the 1980's are not demonstrably different from students of their parents' or grandparents' generation in terms of their knowledge of American history . . . Indeed, given the reduced dropout rate and the less elitist composition of the 17-year-old student body today, one could argue that students today know more American history than did their peers of the past" (787).[7]

To say that schools are doing better than critics claim is also not to put forth the notion that things are fine and we should call off reforms. Too many schools are too boring. Students who come here from Europe to study find American schools easier than their own. This by itself is not compelling because these visiting scholars are certainly not a representative sample of their countries' students. On the other hand, American students studying abroad also find our schools by and large easier.[8] Standards could be ramped up, but they shouldn't be in an atmosphere of pain and punishment, which is what is happening now and has been happening for the last twenty years.

In the meantime, take note that nostalgia is often accompanied by amnesia—we don't remember well the way we were. As an exercise in memory jogging, you might wish to peruse Richard Rothstein's little 1998 book *The Way We Were?*[9]

> *In the meantime, take note that nostalgia is often accompanied by amnesia— we don't remember well the way we were.*

And keep in mind Cremin's summary comment on the situation: "Just about the time Adam first whispered to Eve that they were living through an age of transition, the Serpent doubtless issued the first complaint that academic standards were beginning to decline" (89).

Notes

1. Bell, Terrel. 1989. *The Thirteenth Man*. New York: Free Press.

2. Cremin, Lawrence. 1989. *Popular Education and Its Discontents*. New York: Harper & Row.

3. Tyler, Ralph. 1976. *Perspectives on American Education: Reflections on the Past, Challenges for the Future*. Chicago: Science Research Associates.

4. Raubinger, Frederick M., Harold G. Rowe, Donald Poper, and Charles K. West. 1969. *The Development of Secondary Education*. Toronto: Collier-McMillan.

5. Fine, Benjamin. 1943. "Ignorance of History Shown by College Freshmen." *New York Times*, 4 April, A1.

6. Finn, Chester E. Jr., and Diane Ravitch. 1987. *What Do Our Seventeen-Year-Olds Know?* New York: Harper & Row.

7. Whittington, Dale. 1992. "What Have Our Seventeen-Year-Olds Known in the Past?" *American Educational Research Journal* (winter): 776–78.

8. Loveless, Tom. 2002. *The Brown Center Report on American Education: How Well Are American Students Learning?* Washington, DC: Brookings Institution.

9. Rothstein, Richard. 1998. *The Way We Were?* New York: Century Foundation Press.

14! Hey, Big Spender

What do I say when people say, "America spends more money on its schools than any other nation"?

You can say, "There are at least three ways of calculating school spending and the United States is not highest on any of them. It is high using one method, average using another, and low using a third."

Those who claim we spend more money than any other nation would have a hard time convincing the many parents who spend many hours raising funds for things the school would provide, given an adequate budget. Teachers, who regularly spend their own funds for supplies that should come from the district, would likely remain skeptical as well. It is also curious given the ramshackle condition of so many schools.[1] Back on pages 44–45, I described some of the dreadful physical conditions afflicting some schools. A May 16, 2003, editorial in the *New York Times* observed, "Schools are especially desperate for construction money that would permit them to renovate crumbling school buildings coast to coast"[2] (a Google search on "crumbling schools" in January 2004 yielded 4,460 hits).

A study by the General Accounting Office in 1996 concluded we needed $112 billion to repair and renovate school buildings—more than the Bush administration estimated it needed to rebuild Iraq.[3] By 2000, a more comprehensive survey put the sum at $321 billion.[4] The American Institute of Architects estimated that 60 percent of existing schools need a major repair and the soaring enrollments since 1985 required 36 percent of our schools to use portables.[5] The American Society of Civil Engineers in 2001 rated ten categories of infrastructure and gave its lowest grade (D–) to schools.[6]

If we're lavishing such largesse on the schools, how can such conditions exist?

At least three methods have been used to calculate how much money countries spend on their schools: percent of per capita income, annual expenditure per pupil, and percent of gross domestic product or percent of per capita GDP (both yield the same outcome). None of these techniques finds America spending more money than other nations.

1. *Spending as a percent of per capita income.* This calculation was first made by Edith Rasell and Laurence Mishel of the Economic Policy Institute in 1990.[7] They found that the United States was fourteenth of sixteen developed nations. Neither Rasell nor Mishel nor anyone else has repeated this analysis more recently.

2. *Number of dollars per pupil.* The Organization for Economic Cooperation and Development provides this statistic in its now annual publication, *Education at a Glance.*[8] There are thirty-two nations in OECD. Twenty-four of them provided data for the 2002 edition on the number of dollars spent on elementary schools. The United States ranked third behind Denmark and Switzerland. It also ranked third among the twenty-eight nations with data for secondary school spending, trailing Austria and Switzerland.

I have sometimes said in the past that the United States would be number one in spending if we added in the dollars spent on higher education, but this is not true either. It is true that, after trailing Switzerland for years, the United States now spends more on higher education than any other nation. However, if one tallies all three levels—elementary, secondary, and tertiary—Switzerland spends more overall.

Although OECD uses a conversion—purchasing power parities—that is supposed to equate the systems, it doesn't really work because purchasing power parities don't address issues of quality of life, values, standard of living, and so on. The number of dollars spent per kid per year is not a particularly good indicator, and I provide it here only to show that the United States doesn't spend the most money even using this indicator. (See Figure 14–1.)

Expenditures per Student per Year in U.S. Dollars by Country
(converted using purchasing power parities)

Countries ranked by amount spent on primary education.
Although the report appeared in 2002, the reference year for all
OECD data is 1999.

Rank	Country	Elementary	Secondary
1.	Denmark	6,721	7,626
2.	Switzerland	6,663	9,756
3.	United States	6,582	8,157
4.	Austria	6,568	8,504
5.	Norway	5,920	7,628
6.	Sweden	5,736	5,911
7.	Italy	5,354	6,518
8.	Japan	5,240	6,039
9.	Australia	4,858	6,850
10.	Netherlands	4,162	5,670
11.	France	4,139	7,152
12.	Finland	4,138	5,863
13.	Belgium	3,952	6,444
14.	Germany	3,818	6,603
15.	Spain	3,635	4,864
16.	United Kingdom	3,627	5,608
17.	Portugal	3,478	5,181
18.	Ireland	3,018	4,383
19.	Korea	2,838	3,419
20.	Hungary	2,179	2,368
21.	Greece	2,176	2,904
22	Poland	1,888	1,583
23.	Czech Republic	1,769	4,043
24.	Mexico	1,096	1,480

Source: OECD. *Education at a Glance.* 2002. Paris: OECD.

Figure 14–1. Expenditures per Student per Year in U.S. Dollars

Spending as a Percentage of Gross Domestic Product (elementary and secondary schools combined)

1	Sweden	5.1
2.5*	New Zealand	4.8
2.5	Denmark	4.8
4.5	Norway	4.3
4.5	Portugal	4.3
6	France	4.2
7	Austria	4.1
8	Switzerland	4.0
9.5	Australia	3.8
9.5	Finland	3.8
11	Poland	3.6
12	Belgium	3.5
12	Canada	3.5
12	United States	3.5
15.5	Spain	3.3
15.5	United Kingdom	3.3
17.5	Italy	3.2
17.5	Korea	3.2
20	Ireland	3.1
20	Mexico	3.1
20	Netherlands	3.1
23	Czech Republic	3.0
23	Slovak Republic	3.0
23	Germany	3.0
25.5	Hungary	2.9
25.5	Turkey	2.9
27	Japan	2.7
28	Greece	2.4

*By convention, when the elements being ranked (countries in this case) tie for certain ranks, their ranks are presented as the average of what the ranks would be if they were not tied. Thus, New Zealand and Denmark tie for what would be second and third, and the average of second and third is 2.5. The United States, Belgium, and Canada tie for what would be ranks 11, 12, and 13 if untied, so all three receive the average rank of 12.

Source: OECD. 2002. *Education at a Glance.* Paris: OECD.

Figure 14–2. Spending as a Percentage of Gross Domestic Product

3. *Spending as a percent of gross domestic product (GDP)*. Some have objected to the use of this statistic because some nations have large GDPs and some have small GDPs. In fact, it makes little difference whether one uses GDP or per capita GDP. The most recent edition of *Education at a Glance* (2002) provides education spending for twenty-eight nations, combining elementary and secondary information. The United States spends precisely the same percentage as the average among the twenty-eight nations. If one ranks the nations, the United States also falls in the middle, tying Belgium and Canada for thirteenth place (see Figure 14–2).

OECD also offers data separately for elementary and secondary education. Of the twenty-four nations with data at the elementary level, the United States ties Norway, Portugal, and the United Kingdom for eleventh place. At the secondary level America ties with the United Kingdom and Japan for sixteenth place among the twenty-eight countries for which OECD has data.

Thus, different statistics give different impressions, but the United States never comes off as Daddy Warbucks. I prefer either GDP measure because it seems to me to reflect the amount of a nation's wealth that it is willing to dedicate to its future.

Of course, in addition to looking at how much countries spend on schools, one must also look at where they spend it. In a list of services provided, the United States would likely be number one. For instance, such a list of would probably show that U.S. schools furnish services that many countries do not:

music,
transportation,
meals,
counseling, and, especially,
special education. And . . .
sports.

The often palatial stadia and pools and other athletic facilities found here astonish European exchange students. In Europe, most sports activities transpire in the community and people cheer for local community teams, not for their alma maters.

Notes

1. National Center for Education Statistics (NCES). 1999. *Condition of America's Public School Facilities*. Report No. NCES 2000032. Washington, DC: NCES.

2. "Federal Help for Crumbling Schools." 2003 editorial. *New York Times*, 16 May, A26.

3. General Accounting Office. 1996. *School Facilities: America's Schools Report Differing Conditions*. Report No. GAO/HEHS-96-103. Washington, DC: General Accounting Office.

4. National Education Association. 2000. *Modernizing Our Schools: What Will It Cost?* Washington, DC: National Education Association.

5. Canavan, Robert P. 2001. Testimony before the House Ways and Means Committee. 21 March. Available at *www.modernschools.org /media/7899.html*.

6. American Society of Civil Engineers. 2001. Statement to the Senate Subcommittee on Transportation and Infrastructure. 23 July. Available at *http://epw.senate.gov/107th/asce0721.htm*.

7. Rasell, Edith, and Laurence Mishel. 1990. *Shortchanging Education: How U.S. Spending on Grades K–12 Lags Behind Other Industrialized Nations*. Washington, DC: Economic Policy Institute.

8. Organization for Economic Cooperation and Development (OECD). 2002. *Education at a Glance*. Paris: OECD.

Throwing Money at the Schools

What do I say when people say, "Money doesn't matter. Don't throw money at the schools"?

You can say, "It certainly does matter. Study after study shows that it does. The graphs that claim money does not matter are misleading."

Closely related to the myths that poverty is not an excuse and that America spends more money on its schools than any other nation is the myth that money doesn't matter. You can't cure schools' problems by throwing money at them.

This notion has become something of a mantra of the Bush administration and of the Right generally. In June 2003, a graph on the homepage of the U.S. Department of Education showed federal spending on education from 1966 to a projected figure for 2004 plotted against NAEP reading scores. The Department should have been ashamed to post this piece of propaganda and I am gratified that at least *Education Week* managed to call the department on it. The graph is shown in Figure 15–1.

In *Chance,* a publication of the American Statistical Association, researchers Howard Wainer of the National Board of Medical Examiners and Daniel Koretz of Harvard University explain what is wrong with the graph: "(1) The left-hand axis shows the wrong measure; (2) the right-hand axis uses an inappropriate scale; (3) the impression given is very specific to the subject matter chosen; and (4) the graphic format is unreasonable" (15).[1] Oh, is that *all*?

The left-hand axis shows total federal spending. One could

Federal Spending on K-12 Education under the Elementary and Secondary Education Act (NCLB) and NAEP Reading Scores (Age 9)

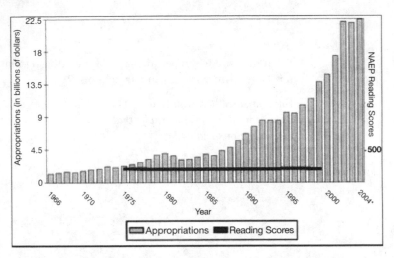

NOTE: Appropriations for NCLB do not include funding for special education.

Source: U.S. Department of Education Budget Service and *NAEP 1999 Trends in Academic Progress*

Figure 15–1. Federal Spending and NAEP Reading Trends

wonder why anyone would use federal spending, which even after the alleged increases accounts for only 7 to 8 percent of spending on education, as the left-hand axis. Even worse, the graph misleads because, since 1985, K–12 enrollments have soared. It would thus be amazing if total expenditures had *not* gone up. What we need is a graph showing per pupil expenditures and when Wainer and Koretz created that, they found growth over time. Finally, the years that show most of the increase in spending are years for which *no test results yet exist.* The greatest growth in spending occurs from 2000 to 2004, but the latest NAEP trend data are from 1999.

The Education Department's graph shows NAEP reading scores on a 500-point scale, but the NAEP reading scales were constructed so that they had a mean of 250 and a standard deviation of 50—*for all three ages tested combined*. This means that most scores would fall between 100 and 400, again for all ages combined (this is a range of plus and minus three standard deviations, and 99.74 percent of all scores would fall in this range). To show scores for a single age on such an enormous scale is wholly misleading.

How convenient for the department that it shows only reading scores, where growth has been slowest. Graphs for math or science would show much more growth.

As for the fourth problem Wainer and Koretz identified, the two *y*-axes—constant dollars on the left, reading scores on the right—are plotted independently. This "allows the plotter (in the pejorative sense), to play any game at all, making the variables shown appear to have whatever relationship is desired" (47). Wainer and Koretz then played games with the graph, manipulating the scales to make it appear that achievement increased as spending lagged and even that achievement increased as spending declined.

The myth that money doesn't matter has always enjoyed widespread belief and one can wonder why no one ever says money doesn't matter to the space program or to the Department of Defense. Indeed, the NASA approach of "bigger, faster, cheaper" apparently played a big roll in the *Columbia* shuttle disaster. Money by itself doesn't put a man on the Moon or send a probe to Mars, but it certainly makes those endeavors possible.

The belief in money's impotence appeared to receive research confirmation from two studies, one in 1989 and another in 1993. The 1993 "study" is a despicable hoax from former Secretary of Education William J. Bennett, so let us scatter it to the winds first. In 1993, Bennett began a series, *Report Card on American Education* through the right-wing American Legislative Exchange Council.[2] The series continues today, but Bennett is no longer the author.

Bennett's claim that money is unrelated to achievement came from matching up state-level SAT scores with state-level spending. Bennett performed no statistical analyses on these indicators. He merely commented that some of the lowest-scoring states spent a lot of money while some of the highest-scoring states spent very little.

Bennett's report attained instant celebrity status with the Right. Pundit and fellow conservative George Will immediately pounced on the data with a column in the *Washington Post,* "Meaningless Money Factor."[3] Will observed that the five states with the highest SAT scores—Iowa, North Dakota, South Dakota, Utah, and Minnesota—were all low spenders. On the other hand, Will said, look at New Jersey. New Jersey spends more money per student per year than any other state and still finished only thirty-ninth in the great SAT race.

Well, the five states Will mentioned score high on any test that is thrown at them, it is true. However, one might have thought that a disinterested analyst might have noticed Mississippi's high rank. On most other tests, Mississippi finishes at or near the bottom. For example, it was forty-eighth for the 2003 NAEP fourth-grade reading assessment. Thirty-six of forty-one nations participating in TIMSS outscored it.

What neither Will nor Bennett bothered to reveal, of course, is that in the highest-scoring states, virtually no one *takes* the SAT. Those are all ACT states. In the year of the study, the percent of seniors taking the SAT in those states was 5, 6, 5, 4, and 10, respectively. Those students wished to attend elite institutions mostly on the East and West Coasts. Indeed, in Iowa, any students finishing with a grade point average in the top half of their classes do not have to take *any* college admission test. They may attend any schools of their choosing in the Iowa state system.

In New Jersey, by contrast, 76 percent of the senior class huddled in angst on Saturday mornings to bubble in answer sheets for the College Board. One might wish to create a cheer, "OK NJ!" for a state that encourages three-quarters of its students to apply to four-year institutions that require the SAT. Of course, when three-fourths of the student body from one state competes against an elite 5 percent from another, the outcome is preordained.

> *Of course, when three-fourths of the student body from one state competes against an elite 5 percent from another, the outcome is preordained.*

I don't know if Will knew about the different participation rates in different states, but Bennett certainly did and that makes his action all the more reprehensible. Bennett's predecessor, Terrel Bell, had created graphs that came to be known as the wall charts.

The wall charts ranked states on a variety of educational outcome variables. But the charts divided states into two categories: SAT states and ACT states. Bennett had to know that the SAT was not a valid measure of state-level achievement (I am quite certain he also knows that ETS and the College Board have maintained over the years that the SAT does not measure achievement, period).

Bennett also likely knew of a study from 1984 that repudiated his contention. Back in 1982, the College Board treated state-level SAT scores like state secrets. Each year regional representatives of the Board would fan out across the states to bring the information to select officials in state departments of education. But in 1982, an enterprising journalist—in Ohio, I think—called all fifty states and obtained their average scores. Then he published them, just as Bennett had done, although I doubt that the reporter realized that his results were affected by the differential participation rates across the states.

These results received considerable media attention and caused considerable consternation as a number of states one would expect to score low did quite well and, conversely, a number of states with generally high test scores fared poorly. Researchers Brian Powell and Lala Carr Steelman straightened things out by adjusting statistically for the different participation rates. They found that variation in participation rates accounted for about 85 percent of the variation in scores among states. They repeated their study in 1996 and reached the same conclusion.[4, 5]

In the latter study, though, they also looked to see how money might influence scores if all states had the same participation rate (a straightforward statistical procedure). They found SAT scores to rise by about fifteen points for every thousand dollars spent above the national average for spending. The SAT is a test remote from the classroom, but even on this distant indicator, money matters.[6]

The 1989 study by Eric Hanushek, then at the University of Rochester, has had a more profound and long-lasting influence no doubt because Hanushek did not publish his findings through a right-wing advocacy organization, but in the respected house organ of the American Educational Research Association, *Educational Researcher.* Hanushek's conclusion is straightforward: "expenditures are not systematically related to student achievement."[7]

Other researchers attacked the study almost immediately, and with good reason. For one thing, Hanushek claimed to have reviewed 187 studies, but only 65 of them actually dealt with money and achievement—and some of those had at best a remote connection to the relationship between spending and achievement. More importantly, Hanushek never said how he reached his verdict. He merely presented the numbers and baldly stated his conclusion. Researchers typically use some kind of decision rule in situations like this.

Independent researcher Keith Baker asked, "If there really is no relationship, how many of the sixty-five studies might we expect to indicate one by chance?" Too many for it to be chance, he concluded. Of the sixty-five studies, thirty-eight showed a positive relationship, while only fourteen pointed to a negative one. The remainder either found no relationship or did not present enough data to permit a conclusion one way or another.[8]

Along with this flaw, Baker also pointed to a significant lapse in logic. Hanushek's analysis dealt with the *level* of achievement that students attained, but his recommendation not to throw money at the schools dealt with *changes* in the level of achievement. Parental background and community characteristics strongly affect level of achievement. Indeed, some readers might recall that after the appearance of *The Coleman Report* in 1966, people wondered if schools had any influence at all independent of family variables (the schools do matter; the cry of "it's all family" was a misinterpretation).

Family and community are less related to *changes* in the level of achievement. Thus, if we were to put more resources in impoverished schools, we might expect to see changes in achievement, although the levels of achievement in those schools might not rise to the levels of achievement attained in more affluent neighborhoods.

Note that Hanushek said there was no *systematic* relationship between spending and achievement. This is a most curious statement because his primitive methodology could not possibly reveal such a relationship even if there were one. Hanushek used a vote-counting technique. If a study finds a positive relationship between money and achievement, that category gets one vote. A negative finding gives a vote to the "no relationship" category, and so forth. To reach a conclusion about a systematic relationship, Hanushek would have needed a much more sophisticated methodology and statistical techniques.

Finally, Baker observed that if Hanushek's contention were true, it would be a cause for shame because it would mean that we were underfunding poor districts. The proper relationship between money and achievement, Baker argued, is negative. He drew a medical analogy:

> Think about hospital costs and dead patients. We would not be surprised to find that patients who die cost more in medical care than those who are cured. Indeed, policy makers guarantee this outcome by making every effort to prolong life . . . A good school resembles a good hospital in that more resources are devoted to treat those who are most difficult to deal with— the sickest patients or the least able students . . . A positive relationship between spending and achievement indicates a failure of the education system to adequately address the needs of disadvantaged students. (629)

In fact, we operate with this logic for one portion of the system: special education. All special education costs more than regular classroom instruction, with the typical multiplier being about 2.5. Yet outcomes are not as good for special education students, in terms of test scores, as they are for regular students.

Other studies have contradicted Hanushek.[9,10,11,12,13,14] Among the most potent of these are the studies by Hedges, Laine, and Greenwald and Krueger.

It is sometimes alleged that students in poor areas receive more money than those in middle-class neighborhoods. A study by Biddle and Berliner refutes this.[15] They looked at the spending on schools compared with how many students in the schools lived in poverty. The results were dramatic and are shown in Figure 15–2. Districts that spend more than ten thousand dollars per student have

> *It is sometimes alleged that students in poor areas receive more money than those in middle-class neighborhoods.*

less than 10 percent of their students living in poverty. Districts that spend five thousand dollars or less per student have more than 20 percent in poverty.

Many people have observed that this kind of inequity is unique to the United States among developed countries. Other nations have transfer policies to eliminate the differences. In the words of Robert Slavin of Johns Hopkins University:

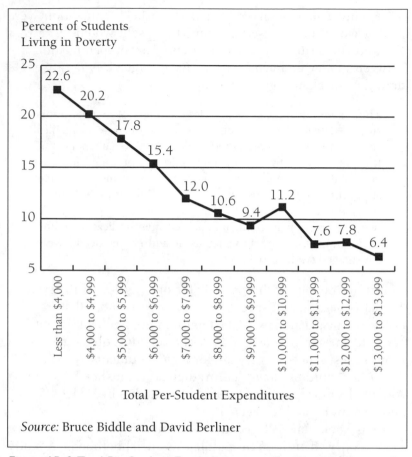

Figure 15–2. Total Per-Student Expenditures as a Function of Percent of Students Living in Poverty

To my knowledge, the U.S. is the only nation to fund elementary and secondary education based on local wealth. Other developed countries either equalize funding [across the states] or provide extra funding for individuals or groups felt to need it. In the Netherlands, for example, national funding is provided to all schools based on the number of pupils enrolled, but for every guilder allocated to a middle-class Dutch child, 1.25 guilders are allocated for a lower-class child and 1.9 guilders for a minority child, exactly the opposite of the situation in the U.S. where lower-class and minority children receive less than middle-class white children. (520)[16]

The myth persists, though, and will likely continue since it seems, like so much from the Right, impervious to data. At the 2003 Milken Institute Global Conference, Robert Lally, president of Leapfrog SchoolHouse, part of Michael Milken's empire known as Knowledge Universe, had this to say: "The more we spend, the reading scores don't improve." Not the most articulate phrasing, but I'm certain the audience knew what he meant.

Notes

1. Wainer, Howard, and Daniel Koretz. 2003. "Political Statistics." *Chance* (fall): 45–47.

2. Bennett, William J. 1993. *Report Card on American Education.* Washington, DC: American Legislative Exchange Council.

3. Will, George F. 1993. "Meaningless Money Factor." *Washington Post,* 24 September, A22.

4. Powell, Brian, and Lala Carr Steelman. 1984. "Variations in State SAT Scores: Meaningful or Misleading?" *Harvard Educational Review* (fall): 389–412.

5. Powell, Brian, and Lala Carr Steelman. 1996. "Bewitched, Bothered and Bewildering: The Use and Misuse of State SAT Scores." *Harvard Educational Review* (spring): 29–59.

6. It is getting less remote all the time as school districts adopt higher SAT scores as a goal in itself. One district has given the PSAT to all of its eighth graders in hopes of finding ways of raising SAT scores. This procedure, giving a test designed for eleventh graders to eighth graders in a low-scoring district, will probably do nothing except further lower the self-esteem of the students.

7. Hanushek, Eric. 1989. "The Impact of Differential Spending on School Performance." *Educational Researcher* (May): 45–51.

8. Baker, Keith. 1991. "Yes, Throw Money at the Schools." *Phi Delta Kappan* (April): 628–30.

9. Wainer, Howard. 1993. "Does Spending Money on Education Help?" *Educational Researcher* (December): 22–24.

10. Ferguson, Ronald. 1991. "Paying for Public Education: New Evidence on How and Why Money Matters." *Harvard Journal on Legislation* 28 (2): 465–98.

11. Hedges, Larry V., Ronald D. Laine, and Rob Greenwald. 1994.

"Does Money Matter? A Meta-Analysis of Studies of the Effects of Differential School Inputs on Student Outcomes." *Educational Researcher* (April): 5–14.

12. Payne, Kevin P., and Bruce Biddle. 1999. "Poor School Funding, Child Poverty, and Mathematics Achievement." *Educational Researcher* (August/September): 5–12.

13. Krueger, Alan B. 1997. "Experimental Estimates of Education Production Functions." Working paper W6051. Washington, DC: National Bureau of Economic Research.

14. Wenglinksy. Harold. 1997. *When Money Matters: How Educational Expenditures Improve Student Performance and How They Don't.* Princeton, NJ: Policy Information Center, Educational Testing Service.

15. Biddle, Bruce, and David C. Berliner. 2002. "A Research Synthesis: Unequal School Funding in the United States." Available at *http://www.ascd.org/publications/ed_lead/200205/biddle.html*.

16. Slavin, Robert. 1999. "How Can Funding Equity Ensure Enhanced Achievement?" *Journal of Educational Finance* 24: 519–29.

16 Public Versus Private Schools

What do I say when people say, "Private schools get better results than public schools"?

You can say, "The differences are small given the differences in who attends the two types of schools and given the advantages that private schools have. When we match parental education levels, the differences disappear."

Comparing public and private schools is much more difficult than the question would make it appear because neither category is monolithic. Some public school critics depict public schools as a government monopoly, implying that they're all as alike as Big Macs. But many districts maintain magnet schools, charter schools, and other special school programs. Districts, particularly at the elementary level, have different programs at different elementary schools and offer parents intradistrict options. Indeed, one 1985 study found so much diversity in high schools that its report was titled *The Shopping Mall High School*.[1]

Similarly, some private schools select and cater to an academic elite—and charge tuition accordingly. Some private schools remain as segregation academies, simply attempting to maintain an all-white clientele. Then there are Catholic and other church-affiliated schools, where education includes indoctrination into a particular religion. Catholic schools have increasingly educated poor urban youth because their traditional clientele has gone elsewhere. In 1960 Catholic schools enrolled 12.6 percent of all students, but currently they account for only 4.9 percent.[2]

Public and private schools do differ on a number of characteristics that can influence achievement. The most obvious of these

characteristics, of course, is selectivity.
Private schools can and do have selection criteria. Using selection criteria,
private schools end up with fewer
English Language Learners, fewer children eligible for free and reduced-price
meals, fewer special education students, and fewer minorities.

To the extent that small schools and small classes help
achievement, private schools have a leg up on public schools.
According to the National Center for Education Statistics
(NCES), Catholic schools, which account for 48 percent of all private school enrollments, average about 300 students per school,
while other religious schools and nonsectarian schools each average around 142.[3] ("Forty-eight percent of all private school
enrollments" means 5 percent of all enrollments.) As for student–teacher ratios, public schools come in at 15.6 to 1, private
schools 13.2 to 1. Some 36 percent of private schools have student–teacher ratios of less than 10 to 1 while only 10 percent of
public schools attain this figure.[4]

In part because they are larger, public schools have more
diverse offerings than private schools. Only 18 percent of private
schools have a separate gifted and talented program, compared
with 68 percent of public schools. At the high school level, public schools are more likely to offer courses for college credit,
advanced placement, work-based learning, vocational preparation, and career academies (National Center for Education
Statistics 2003, 8). However, a higher proportion of students in
private schools complete advanced-level courses.

Two reports have infused private schools with an aura of
superiority in the realm of achievement. There were Coleman,
Hoffer, and Kilgore's *High School Achievement: Public, Catholic and
Private Schools Compared*[5] and John Chubb and Terry Moe's
Politics, Markets and America's Schools.[6] Coleman's earlier work,
Equality of Educational Opportunity, had established him as a dom-
inant figure in educational policy. Thus, when the later work
arrived, people were prepared to listen.

Coleman's comparisons and other reports gave private
schools and Catholic schools especially an aura of achievement,
sometimes to the point of adulation. Coleman cautioned against
such to little avail: "One should not make a mistake: our esti-

mates for the size of the private sector effects show them to be small."[7]

Others were not so reticent. Nina Shokraii (now Nina Shokraii Rees) at the Heritage Foundation explained in a "research" essay why Catholic schools spell success for America's inner-city children.[8] Diane Ravitch answered for *Forbes* readers the question, Why do Catholic schools succeed?[9] *Investor's Business Daily* took a most unbusinesslike attitude, referring to Catholic schools' "magic."[10]

When Chubb and Moe's book came along, the stage had been set for it to play a major role. The Reagan and first Bush administrations had been pushing vouchers and tuition tax credits. As part of that agenda, both had adopted the strategy of never saying anything positive about American public education. In addition, two years into Reagan's first term, the Department of Education had dropped *A Nation at Risk* and its attendant publicity on the country. While Coleman's report was read mostly by scholars, *A Nation at Risk* was written to be accessible to the layman. It made a case, albeit a distorted one, that the nation's public schools were indeed in crisis, and when the Chubb and Moe analysis arrived seven years later, people had already begun talking about alternatives to public schools.

Chubb and Moe argued that school effectiveness was influenced by how schools were organized. Private schools were organized like businesses and that made them more efficient than the public schools, which they didn't call government schools but "institutions of direct democratic control," a term somewhat more benign:

> America's public schools are governed by institutions of direct democratic control, and their organizations should be expected to bear the indelible stamp of those institutions. They should tend to be highly bureaucratic and systematically lacking in the requisites of effective performance. Private schools, on the other hand, operate in a very different institutional setting distinguished by the basic features of markets—decentralization, competition and choice—and their organizations should be expected to bear a very different stamp as a result. They should tend to possess autonomy, clarity of mission, strong leadership, and team cooperation that the public schools want, but . . . are unlikely to have. (67)

This description is straightforward. Much of the other exposition is not. It conjures up a miracle-working effect from choice: "Choice is a self contained reform with its own rationale and justification. It has the capacity *all by itself* to bring about the kind of transformation that, for years, reformers have been seeking to engineer" (217). Reading Chubb and Moe's paean to choice, the late Harold Howe accused them of treating choice as the eighth wonder of the world (79).[11]

That Chubb and Moe should find such transformational effects is all the more odd because they used high school and beyond (HSB) data. Most analysts looking at these data have noticed immediately that the signal feature of them is that they show so little growth from grade 10 to grade 12 for either public or private schools. The tests focused largely on skills learned before high school. Why would anyone expect them to show much change in the final years?

John Witte at the University of Wisconsin observed that the gain from grade 10 to grade 12 was .2 of a standard deviation. The learning rate in the first seven grades is closer to 1.0 standard deviations. Given that high school covers a lot of content, .2 standard deviation seems extremely small—unless one is measuring something one doesn't expect to change in the high school years.[12]

Beyond all that, it is not at all clear how Chubb and Moe massaged their data. Many a researcher has suffered headaches trying to determine what methods they actually used. This condition, of course, would leave education reporters with only one decision: since the reporters wouldn't be able to figure out the analyses either, they would simply have to decide whether or not to trust the researchers. Because both Chubb and Moe were at the time residents of the relatively prestigious Brookings Institution, a think tank at the time erroneously perceived as liberal, most chose to trust them (*Education Week* finessed the issue of data by publishing a several-thousand-word excerpt that didn't contain any on June 6, 1990).

Others were more skeptical. David Berliner and Bruce Biddle, in *The Manufactured Crisis,* observed that Chubb and Moe "covered their tracks quite well, however, with vigorous rhetoric, extensive but slanted reviews of historical and comparative materials and—crucially—by drawing artful but questionable conclusions from analyses of HSB data" (120).[13]

In *Rethinking School Choice: Limits of the Market Metaphor,* Jeffrey Henig, then of George Washington University (now Columbia University), took Chubb and Moe to task for using roundabout methods to obscure their findings: the gains between tenth and twelfth grades were small, as were the differences between public and private schools.[14] Similarly, Peter Cookson, then of Delphi and now of Columbia University, made the same critical point:

> Their key variable, which they call school organization, is so comprehensive as to be incomprehensible . . . The authors have so magnified their results by altering the unit of analysis from a score to a time frame, that they have lost sight of their own finding, which indicates that there are very few achievement gains between the sophomore and the senior year . . . I think it fair to say that Chubb and Moe's argument that student achievement is directly linked to school organization must be taken with an analytic grain of salt. (85–86)[15]

Finally, we return to John Witte for a fair and quantitative take on the Chubb-Moe analysis:

> The Chubb and Moe study is anomalous in many regards. The empirical evidence they offer is drawn entirely from HSB. They disregard much of the prior research that established cautions, limitations and standard practices observed by prior researchers using HSB data. Second, unlike other studies that base policy recommendations on inferences drawn from differences in achievement outcomes in public and private schools, *they never directly test the differential effect of public and private schools on achievement* . . .
>
> Direct estimates of substantive relevance are difficult given the uninterpretable dependent variable they use. By making several simple assumptions, however, I estimate that, if one could modify a school's organization enough to move it from the median school, to the 84th percentile [or school organization], students in the school would, on average, get a fraction of one more item correct out of 115 items on the test. That is a small effect for an enormous change in organizational effectiveness. (118, emphasis in the original)[16]

I spent a lot of time presenting critiques of the Chubb-Moe analysis, even though the book amounts to very little, because it received a great deal of attention when it appeared in 1990. As should be clear by now, though, in terms of positive reports, we are dealing with faith, ideology, or politics. Since no one actually understood how the authors of the research had analyzed the data, on what other basis could one accept the conclusions?

If we look at public-private achievement differences on a test of some integrity, such as NAEP, we do find differences in scores, but these are confounded with other differences such as parental education level. In addition, a variable such as parental education level is based on reports of the students, and the students clearly think that their parents have more education than they do. Currently, a little more than one-quarter of adults have at least a bachelor's degree. Yet on the 2003 NAEP results for eighth graders, 70 percent of those in Catholic schools, 79 percent of those in other private schools, and 46 percent of those in public schools reported that their parents had completed college.

> When adjusted for parental education level, the differences between public and private schools are either small or nonexistent.

The results from the one study that controlled for parental education are shown in Figure 16–1. As can be seen, when adjusted for parental education level, the differences between public and private schools are either small or nonexistent.

From Chubb and Moe and from other market theorists, Richard Rothstein of the Economic Policy Institute, Martin Carnoy of Stanford University, and Luis Benveniste of the World Bank derived six hypotheses about the advantages we should see when comparing private versus public schools:

1. Private school personnel are more accountable to parents than are public school personnel.
2. Private schools have more clearly defined expectations and outputs than do public schools.
3. Private elementary schools teach good behavior and values better than public elementary schools.
4. Private schools' teacher selection and retention practices are more efficient than those of public schools.
5. Private schools achieve academic success with curricular

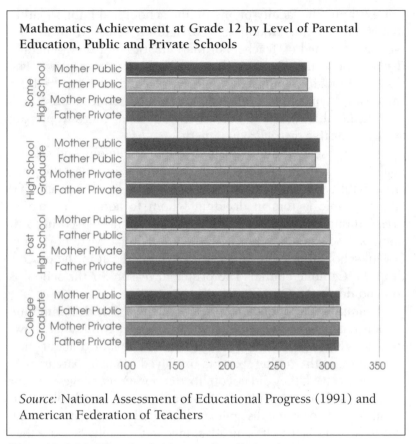

Mathematics Achievement at Grade 12 by Level of Parental Education, Public and Private Schools

Source: National Assessment of Educational Progress (1991) and American Federation of Teachers

Figure 16–1. Mathematics Achievements—Parental

materials (in standard subjects) that do not differ from curricular materials in public schools.

6. Private school innovations stimulate improved practices at the public schools with which they compete.[17]

The team confirmed none of the six hypotheses and in most cases, reality turned out to be much more complex than market-theory conjectures would lead one to expect. For instance, in the case of hypothesis 2, about the clarity of goals, the researchers often found what they called "multiple clarities." A faculty of either a public school or a private school might have a crystal-clear set of goals and expectations. The central administration, on the other hand, might have an equally clear, but contradictory set.

For example, the faculty of one public school had built a mathematics curriculum around the curriculum standards from the National Council of Teachers of Mathematics and they generally disdained teaching the skills that standardized tests measure. The district, though, administered and emphasized the results from the CTBS, a typical norm-referenced standardized test, and teachers felt they had to abandon their own goals at times to prepare students for this district requirement.

In the case of church-affiliated schools, religious and secular goals often clashed. In one Catholic school, for instance, the principal, with twice as many applicants as seats, wanted to emphasize academic factors in deciding whom to admit. The parish priest, though, pressured the principal to admit low-scoring students whose parents were parishioners, saying, "We're not a successful school if our students get into Harvard but in the process drop the Catholic church. The principal reason for the school is to hand down the Catholic religion."

Examining accountability, the researchers found community income characteristics overwhelmed the type of governance. Low-income schools, both public and private, complained about their difficulties with getting parents involved. When parents did become involved, they did not often offer questions, suggestions, or complaints about curriculum or instruction, but complaints about a child's grade or some disciplinary action taken against the child. Private schools had a bit of an advantage in this arena because they could make parental involvement a condition of admission (an advantage also enjoyed by some charter schools). Recent studies have found that parents in low-income neighborhoods lack the kinds of social networks that would permit them to get involved with schools in the same ways as middle-class parents do.[18]

Teachers in more affluent public schools reported a barrage of parent inquiries and suggestions. Parents in these districts felt that they had both a right and a responsibility to participate actively in their children's education. One school even started a weekly newsletter to keep up with the flow of input from parents.

According to Milton Friedman and his acolytes, this is not how it's supposed to work. Private schools, because they must compete for customers, should be more accountable. Yet Rothstein, Carnoy, and Benveniste found that private schools made it clear to parents that matters of curriculum and instruction were reserved to the faculty and administration. In one school, "The proprietors have maintained a clear policy of discouraging parental involvement to prevent interference in the school's operation. Until recently, and for most of the school's 28-year existence, there has been no parent association or other parent advisory group and no invitations for parents to assist in classrooms." Another private school had a simple statement on accountability: *caveat emptor.*

The researchers concluded that their results did not resemble what a Milton Friedman–type economist would predict but did flow from the work of another economist, Byron Brown. Brown argues that schools *must* tend to resemble each other because of the uncertainty of the postschool years. Neither the school—be it public or private—nor the parents can know for sure what the future will bring in terms of employment prospects or further education. Therefore, the schools offer similar curricula and teach in similar ways. A school that is truly a "break-the-mold-school, that deviates too much from the general perception of what a school is, increases the risk that the parents have made the wrong choice by sending their kids there."[19] Although not operating from any economic theory, several researchers evaluating charter schools in Michigan noticed how similar they were to regular public schools and concluded that parents would not risk sending children to a school that was too "far out" from the norm.

This analysis seems to have some history on its side. Summerhill has been much written about, but little imitated. Chris Whittle's Edison Schools, while promising some differences in curriculum (classic texts rather than basals, project-based science, etc.) pitched its ads chiefly with a promise to do better than traditional public schools in the traditional arenas of academic achievement. And in 1932, the Progressive Education Association was able to introduce many innovations into schools only after receiving assurances from colleges and universities that the colleges and universities would not evaluate the graduates of the Progressive schools using the traditional admissions criteria.

> *Private schools, because they must compete for customers, should be more accountable. Yet Rothstein, Carnoy, and Benveniste found that private schools made it clear to parents that matters of curriculum and instruction were reserved to the faculty and administration.*

One study that seemed to find Catholic schools superior to public schools attributed the difference to the presence of a "voluntary community" where parents "make life easier for the schools by insuring that students attend regularly, do their homework, and adhere to the school's behavioral standards" (305).[20]

Rothstein, Carnoy, and Benveniste challenge this conclusion and believe it was reached because those researchers looked only at Catholic schools. Had they looked at all schools, they might have seen what Rothstein, Carnoy, and Benveniste report:

> There were certainly parents with whom we spoke, and about whom the faculty we interviewed spoke, where such characterizations (of a voluntary community) applied. But we did not observe these to be particularly more frequent in private or in Catholic schools as a whole. Rather, in this respect as in so many others, the social, cultural, and economic backgrounds of the parents and the community in which the school was located seemed to be the main determinant of variation, much more so than a school's public or private character or, within the latter group, whether it was religious or secular. Within particular communities, the similarities between schools and the problems they confronted overwhelmed the differences. (66–67)

A far less rigorous study led to a surprising conclusion—surprising to those who commissioned the study, that is. If you live in a suburb and send your child to a private school, "Here's the bottom line: You are probably wasting your hard-earned money."[21] That was the conclusion of a *Money* magazine article, which found American public schools full of "topnotch teachers, challenging courses, and an environment that is conducive to learning. What many public schools are lacking is a student body brimming with kids eager to take advantage of what the school has to offer." Although studies are lacking, these days, the feeling abroad in the land is that this situation of student disengagement has only increased in the decade since *Money's* study.

If you live in a suburb and send your child to a private school, "Here's the bottom line: You are probably wasting your hard-earned money."

Notes

1.Powell, Arthur G., Eleanor Farrar, and David K. Cohen. 1999. *The Shopping Mall High School*. New York: Houghton Mifflin.

2.Brimelow, Peter. 2000. "Private School Surge." *Forbes* (27 November): 104.

3. National Center for Education Statistics. 2003. *Private Schools: A Brief Portrait*.

4. Keep in mind that student–teacher ratios include all certified teachers whether or not they are teaching, and these ratios are not the same as class size. Average class size for the reported ratios in public schools is 23 in elementary schools and 26 in high schools.

5. Coleman, James S., Thomas Hoffer, and Sally Kilgore. 1982. *High School Achievement: Public, Catholic and Private Schools Compared*. New York: Basic Books.

6. Chubb, John, and Terry Moe. 1990. *Politics, Markets, and America's Schools*. Washington, DC: Brookings Institution.

7. Coleman, James S. 1981. "Response to Paige and Keith." *Educational Researcher* (August/September).

8. Shokraii, Nina. 1997. "Why Catholic Schools Spell Success for America's Inner-City Children." Available at *www.heritage.org/Research /UrbanIssues/BG1128.cfm*.

9. Ravitch, Diane. 1996. "Why Do Catholic Schools Succeed?" *Forbes* (7 October).

10. "The Magic of Catholic Schools." 1999. *Investor's Business Daily*, 25 January.

11. Howe, Harold II. 1994. *Thinking About Our Kids: An Agenda for American Education*. New York: Free Press.

12. Cited in Rothman, Robert. 1990. "Paper Launches Academic Attack on Chubb-Moe Book on Education." *Education Week*, 14 November, 19. *Note:* Article was not in the online *Education Week* archive. It was obtained from an editor at the publication.

13. Berliner, David C., and Bruce Biddle. 1994. *The Manufactured Crisis*. Reading, MA: Addison-Wesley.

14. Henig, Jeffrey. 1994. *Rethinking School Choice: Limits of the Market Metaphor*. Princeton, NJ: Princeton University Press.

15. Cookson, Peter. 1994. *School Choice: The Struggle for the Soul of American Education*. New Haven: Yale University Press.

16. Witte, John. 1992. "Private Versus Public School Achievement: Are There Findings That Should Affect the Educational Choice Debate?" *Economics of Education Review* (December): 371–94.

17. Rothstein, Richard, Martin Carnoy, and Luis Benveniste. 1999. *Can Public Schools Learn from Private Schools? Case Studies in the Public and Private Sectors*. Washington, DC: Economic Policy Institute. A slightly different version was published by Routledge Falmer Institute in 2001 as *All Else Equal: Are Public and Private Schools Different?* with Benveniste as lead author.

18. Horvat, Erin McNamara, Elliot B. Weininger, and Annette Lareau. 2003. "From Social Ties to Social Capital: Class Differences in the Relations Between Schools and Parent Networks." *American Educational Research Journal* (summer): 319–51.

19. Brown, Byron. 1997. "Why Governments Run Schools." *Economics of Education Review* 11: 287–300.

20. Bryk, Anthony, Valerie E. Lee, and Peter B. Holland. 1993. *Catholic Schools and the Common Good*. Cambridge, MA: Harvard University Press.

21. Topolnicki, Denise M. 1994. "Why Private Schools Are Rarely Worth the Money." *Money* (October): 98–112.

17 Hanging In or Dropping Out?

What do I say when people say, "The dropout rate is
terrible and getting worse"?

*You can say, "You might be right. Ironically, the very
attempt to raise standards is the likely culprit."*

his is the one chapter of the book where I reach a different conclusion than in the original. Then I wrote, "You can say
dropout rates are improving and have been for a number of
years."

That might have been true in 1996, when the book was constructed. The real impact of high-stakes tests was yet to be felt.
Even then I began with, "We must admit at the outset that the
dropout rate is one of the squishiest statistics we have in all of education." That remains true. We do have new information on
dropouts that reveals a higher rate (at the same time, we have the
Houston debacle to make us anxious about the veracity of any
reported rates). Now, instead of seeing headlines about completion
rates rising, we see "Tougher Standards for Exit Exams May Close
Off Options for Kids Who Fail" (Stacy Vanek Smith, *Christian
Science Monitor*, October 21, 2003) and "High School Dropout
Rate Rises and Levy Fears New Test Will Bring Huge Surge"
(Anemona Hartocollis, *New York Times*, February 28, 2001).

In Texas, to obtain the state's highest rank, a district must
report a dropout rate of less than 1 percent. Having worked in a
district with a dropout rate of just over 2 percent—a combination
of wealth, parental education, and high expectations from both

parents and school staff—I know how tough, nigh impossible, such a rate is. Houston was approaching that rate. Its dropout target when the scandal unfolded was 1.5 percent.

As it turned out, the Houston Miracle was how long the district was able to maintain the illusion. Virtually everyone had to have been in on it until one assistant principal blew the whistle and started a scandal sufficiently large to attract *60 Minutes II*.[1] One high school, for example, contained more than a thousand ninth graders but fewer than three hundred seniors. Yet it reported a zero dropout rate. Texas uses about thirty "leaver" codes, many of which do not result in the departed students being labeled dropouts, but even so, Houston showed immense creativity with its numbers. Another high school reported sending all of its graduates to college even though only about 55 percent of its seniors took the SAT and they had a *combined* verbal and math score around 750 (the national combined average for 2003 was 1026). But, after all, Houston was home to the district's role model, Enron.

> *As it turned out, the Houston Miracle was how long the district was able to maintain the illusion.*

Although hardly the most scientific approach, a Google search on "rising dropout rate" produced 100 hits, and "rising dropout rates," 161. Searches on "falling dropout rate" and "falling dropout rates" produced only 13 and 30, respectively. Some of those items discussing falling rates referred to the 1970s and 1980s, when dropout rates were falling, and some contrasted those earlier falling rates with current rising rates. Many of the articles I uncovered dealt with local or state problems, but the geographic coverage was extensive, and not limited to the United States (Kenya, China, Tajikistan, the United Kingdom, and southeastern Europe also turned up). More than a few referenced problems with immigrants or limited English Hispanics.

Part of the problem in understanding the true dropout rate comes from the fact that different states, or in some cases, different districts within a state, count in different ways. When Senator Jeff Bingaman became interested in dropouts in the mid-1990s, he found that only twenty-three states tracked which students left schools.

Economist, and at the time *New York Times* education columnist, Richard Rothstein put it this way: "With so much attention

paid to test scores, an equally important gauge of school performance has mostly been overlooked. High school dropout rates seem
to have jumped. Although dropouts are notoriously hard to track,
the best available data show that in 1990, 26 percent of American
adolescents failed to graduate from high school. By 2000, the
figure had risen to 30 percent."[2]

Urban areas bear the brunt of the rising rate: "The dropout
problem is most severe in the big cities. Crushing social problems
and poor academic preparation often eliminate huge percentages
of students from the rolls before they graduate."[3] As noted later,
social problems and poor academic preparation are not the only
things that conspire to reduce the rolls, according to *Washington
Post* writer Michael Fletcher.

As if tracking students were not hard enough in any atmosphere, the current environment of high-stakes testing and high
anxiety offers schools a variety of incentives for not finding them:
the schools' test scores will be higher and their test passing rates
will be higher, as will their graduation rates. In Texas, students
were pushed into "alternative education" and encouraged to
enroll in GED programs. These actions both exclude the students
from the Texas tests and from being counted as dropouts. As
noted, Texas might have a record number of school leaver
codes—thirty—and many of those do not result in leavers being
classified as dropouts. In New York City, "school officials are
encouraging students to leave regular high school programs even
though they are of school age or have a
right to receive appropriate literacy,
support, and educational services
through the public schools."[4]

Birmingham, Alabama, expelled
522 students, citing their "lack of interest" in school. Curiously, the expulsion
occurred just before the students were
to sit for the state test. When a teacher
called attention to this action, the dis-
trict fired him. He established his own school for these 522 and
now others pushed from the system.

> Birmingham, Alabama,
> expelled 522 students, citing
> their "lack of interest" in
> school. Curiously, the
> expulsion occurred just
> before the students were to
> sit for the state test.

When Walter Haney of Boston College examined high school
graduation rates for the state of New York, he found a decline in
virtually every year from 1987–1988 through 2001–2002. The

yearly falloff was small, but over the eleven-year period, the rate fell from 66.3 percent to 57.6 percent, which left New York ranked forty-fifth in the nation.[5]

Haney used a common method of calculating graduation rates: dividing the number of graduates for a given class by the number of ninth graders three and a half years earlier. Jay Greene and Greg Forster of the Manhattan Institute uses a somewhat more complex—and probably more precise—method than Haney, but their figures are similar to Haney's, generally in the range of plus or minus two percentage points. Greene's figures come from the U.S. Department of Education's Common Core of Data.[6]

Because virtually all states retain a disproportionate number of ninth graders in grade, Greene and Forster averaged the enrollments for grades 8, 9, and 10. This technique likely increases the estimated graduation rate and that could be problematical since retention in grade, especially a high school grade, greatly increases the probability that a student will drop out.

Greene and Forster also estimated how much the population has changed over the four-year period of high school, important where school populations are increasing or decreasing. They do not count GED recipients as graduates. They argue that those seeking a GED are dropouts who have made individual decisions to pursue an alternative route to become certified. Some would disagree. Greene and Forster have conducted their analysis for only two years and thus has little in the way of trend data, but their most recent cross-sectional analysis puts the national graduation rate at 71 percent, with a range from 93 percent (Iowa) to 54 percent (Georgia).

Haney was appalled at the New York differences in graduation rates among ethnicities—74.4 percent for whites, 36.3 percent for blacks, and 33.6 percent for Hispanics. Greene and Forster's New York figures are hardly satisfying, but not quite so stark: 77 percent, 47 percent, and 43 percent, respectively.

Not all states have the capacity to provide data by ethnicity and some have insufficient numbers of some groups to generate a reliable estimate. Greene and Forster could calculate white graduation rates for forty-two states. Again, Iowa and Georgia bracketed the top and bottom, 95 percent and 62 percent, respectively.

For blacks, among thirty-nine states, West Virginia and

Massachusetts led the way with 71 percent and 70 percent, respectively, while Wisconsin and Minnesota fell to the bottom, 40 percent and 43 percent, respectively. Those are not typos. The African American communities in these states have not had as much success in building a middle class as those in, say, North Carolina (55 percent) or Virginia (64 percent).

Among the thirty-nine states that provided data for Hispanics, Montana and Louisiana were tops, with 82 and 70 percent, respectively. Georgia and Alabama came in last with 32 percent and 33 percent, respectively. In the heavily Hispanic southern tier, Arizona ranked thirty-first with a 55 percent graduation rate; Florida, twenty-sixth with 52 percent; California, twenty-second with 55 percent; and New Mexico, thirteenth with 58 percent.

New York has recently begun a program to reach dropouts and pushouts with ads in twenty-seven papers urging them to "reconnect with schools." No word yet on results and one might wonder at the efficiency of using print media to reach students who likely have reading difficulties.

In its landmark 1954 decision, *Brown v. Board of Education*, the Supreme Court wrote,

> Today, education is perhaps the most important function of state and local governments. Compulsory school attendance laws and the great expenditures for education both demonstrate our recognition of the importance of education to our democratic society. It is required in the performance of our most basic public responsibilities, even service in the armed forces. It is the very foundation of good citizenship. Today it is a principal instrument in awakening the child to cultural values, in preparing him for later professional training, and in helping him adjust normally to his environment. In these days, it is doubtful that any child may reasonably be expected to succeed in life if he is denied the opportunity of an education.

The words sound so contemporary. Yet they were written a half century ago, a time when a strong back and a deft hand could still earn a respectable living, a time only six years after the computer had been invented and when people were uncertain about its practical utility.

Today, in the information society, the knowledge worker soci-

> *Today, in the information society, the knowledge worker society, a dropout's prospects are worse than when the Supreme Court ruled segregation laws unconstitutional.*

ety, a dropout's prospects are worse than when the Supreme Court ruled segregation laws unconstitutional.

The United States incarcerates a much larger proportion of its citizens than any other developed nation. Some 702 people of every 100,000 are in jail. The next highest rate occurs in England and Wales, with 139 out of every 100,000. In France, it's 85, Japan, 52. Some of our prison inmates graduated from college. Most of them are dropouts. (See *www.sentencingproject.org/pdfs/pub9036.pdf.*)

Notes

1. "The Texas Miracle." *60 Minutes II.* 7 January 2004. Dan Rather, correspondent.

2. Rothstein, Richard. 2002. "Dropout Rate Is Climbing and Likely to Go Higher." *New York Times,* 9 October, B8.

3. Fletcher, Michael A. 2001. "Progress on Dropout Rate Stalls." *Washington Post,* 2 March, A1.

4. Gotbaum, Betsy. 2002. *Pushing Out At-Risk Students: An Analysis of High School Discharge Figures.* New York: Public Advocate for the City of New York and Advocates for Children, November.

5. Haney, Walt. 2003. "Attrition of Students from New York Schools." Testimony delivered to the New York Senate Standing Committee on Education, 23 September.

6. Greene, Jay P., and Greg Forster. 2003. *Public High School Graduation and College Readiness Rates in the United States.* New York: Manhattan Institute.

Afterword

To steal a line from Kurt Vonnegut, so it goes. These chapters, taken together, have painted a picture of American schools in substantially brighter hues than one limned by critics. Things are much better than the critics contend, except where they're worse: in high-poverty schools, which, because poverty leans disproportionately on black and Hispanic kids, means many schools attended by those two minorities.

But the fear mongers are still out there. CNN host Lou Dobbs, most known lately for his strident opposition to the outsourcing of jobs, had not one but two series on the failure of American education, saying in one that "America's schools are going to hell in a handbasket."[1] In similar fashion, an *Education Week* commentary by Mike Cohen, former education adviser to Bill Clinton and currently president of the standards-mad Achieve; Checker Finn, head of the Thomas B. Fordham Foundation, who once agreed to give a speech at George Mason University only if I were not in the room; and the perpetually Pollyannaish Kati Haycock, director of the Education Trust, declared our high school diplomas worthless.[2] We've got to do more—higher standards *über alles*—in order for students to become workers who can make it in this complex technological world.

It is worth observing that in this capitalist superpower country, no one *ever* talks about how schools should work to improve the quality of our capitalists. The capitalists want workers, docile and low paid preferably, but if schools concentrated on developing the capitalist mentality, the schools would be creating people to compete with the existing capitalists, the last thing the capitalists, for all their singing the praises of competition, want.

Twas ever thus. In 1897, social reformer Jane Addams wrote,

> The businessman has, of course, not said to himself, "I will
> have the public school train office boys and clerks for me, so

that I may have them cheap," but he has thought and sometimes said, "Teach the children to write legibly, to figure accurately and quickly, to acquire habits of punctuality and order; to
be prompt to obey and not question why."[3]

It's an old tactic. If you can make people fear for their future,
you can control them. You can direct them to do what you want,
whether or not it really affects their
future. Apparently, none of these panic
purveyors has ever noticed something:
as a technology matures, it makes life
easier for everyone who uses it.

> *It's an old tactic. If you can make people fear for their future, you can control them.*

Think about cameras. I started in
the 1950s with ones that needed separate light meters. As a begin-
ner, if what I was shooting wasn't static, the phenomenon, say a
sunset, would be over before all the calculations were in. In the
1970s, the through-the-lens meters on my single-lens reflex cameras read the light for me, leaving me free to fiddle with only f-
stops and shutter speeds. In the 1980s, my point-and-shoot
model removed even those considerations unless I chose to over-
ride its automatic settings. I haven't bothered to go digital yet, but
I'm sure you're aware that with digitals you actually see what the
picture will look like before you take it. Better, faster, and easier,
not harder.

Ditto computers. When I replaced my secretary's IBM
Selectric III typewriter with a PC and word-processing package in
1987, she thought she'd died and gone to heaven. Imagine, being
able to press a few keys and correct and revise a document without having to retype the whole damn thing! I learned how to program computers in 1961 and made very, very good money—
allowing for inflation, more than twice what I make these days—
writing simple programs and running canned programs during
my grad school years. I did think that maybe Stanford owed me a
degree in documentation reading along with the one in psychology, maybe in documentation as a foreign language. The documentation that accompanied most software those days was so
dense most people couldn't understand it. By comparison, today's
plug-and-play machines and software-for-dummies documentation are models of ease and clarity.

The Cohen, Finn, and Haycock canon is predicated on the

assumption that everyone must know certain things. But when the TIMSS final year numbers hit the papers, Robert Samuelson of *Newsweek* and the *Washington Post* pointed out that only 4 percent of the labor force actually *needs* advanced math.[4] And in "The Socrates Syndrome," David Campbell argued compellingly that there are very few things that *everyone* needs to know.[5] This is *not* an argument for not learning. Indeed, the future is so unpredictable—only death is certain now that you can beat taxes with a shrewd lawyer or by giving up your citizenship—that your best strategy is to learn everything you can about everything you can because you don't know—can't know—what you'll need.

Surely we can do better by our schools and students. Work for continuous improvement, said Deming, while condemning all forms of punitive accountability and evaluation. No one would suggest that we're approaching the upper asymptote of achievement. But, look back to page 32 and those twenty-two crucially important personal characteristics that tests don't—can't—measure and in your work balance those against the fear mongers' obsession with ever higher test scores.

Notes

1. Dobbs, Lou. 2003. "Wasted Minds: Our Failing Schools." CNN, 4–8 November.

2. Cohen, Michael, Chester E. Finn Jr., and Kati Haycock. 2004. "Creating a High School Diploma That Counts." *Education Week* (10 March): 52.

3. Quoted in Curti, Merle. 1961. *The Social Ideas of American Educators*. Patterson, NJ: Littlefield, Adams.

4. Samuelson, Robert. 1998. "Stupid Students, Smart Economy?" *Washington Post,* 12 March, A15.

5. Campbell, David. 1997. "The Socrates Syndrome." *Phi Delta Kappan* (April): 640–42.